PYRAMID ROCK

HOLIDAY CLUB RESOURCE MATERIAL FOR 5 TO 11s

© Dave Godfrey 2005
First published 2005
ISBN 1 84427 139 0

Scripture Union, 207–209 Queensway, Bletchley, Milton Keynes, MK2 2EB, UK
Email: info@scriptureunion.org.uk
Website: www.scriptureunion.org.uk

Scripture Union Australia, Locked Bag 2, Central Coast Business Centre, NSW 2252 Australia
Website: www.scriptureunion.org.au

Scripture Union USA, PO Box 987, Valley Forge, PA19482, USA
Website: www.scriptureunion.org

All rights reserved. No part of this publication may be reproduced, stored in a retrieval system or transmitted in any form or by any means, electronic, mechanical, photocopying, recording or otherwise, without the prior permission of Scripture Union.

Scripture Union grants permission for pages marked 'Photocopiable' to be copied in the context of a **PYRAMID ROCK** club.

The right of Dave Godfrey to be identified as the author of this work has been asserted by him in accordance with the Copyright, Designs and Patents Act 1988.

Bible quotations have been taken from the Contemporary English Version © American Bible Society. Anglicisations © British and Foreign Bible Society 1996. Published by HarperCollins*Publishers* and used with permission.

British Library Cataloguing-in-Data
A catalogue for this book is available from the British Library.

Cover design by Kevin Wade of kwgraphicdesign
Cover illustration by Toni Goffe
Internal illustrations by Andy Robb
Printed and bound by Progress Print, Malta

The **PYRAMID ROCK** website – www.scriptureunion.org.uk/pyramidrock
Visit the **PYRAMID ROCK** website to access downloadable versions of the photocopiable resources and the memory verse song, to read about other people's experiences and check the advice given by other users on the bulletin board. Additional resources are also available on the **PYRAMID ROCK DVD**.

PYRAMID ROCK is part of *eye level*, Scripture Union's project to catch up with children and young people who have not yet caught sight of Jesus.

Scripture Union is an international Christian charity working with churches in more than 130 countries, providing resources to bring the good news of Jesus Christ to children, young people and families and to encourage them to develop spiritually through the Bible and prayer.

As well as our network of volunteers, staff and associates who run holidays, church-based events and school Christian groups, we produce a wide range of publications and support those who use our resources through training programmes.

FOR TIMOTHY – MY FAVOURITE, AND ONLY, SON OF MY FAVOURITE WIFE!

FOR THE CHILDREN OF THE KIDS ROCK CLUB, WHO ARE DISCOVERING MORE ABOUT JESUS EVERY WEEK.

FOREWORD

PYRAMID ROCK is written for use with children between the ages of 5 and 11, and is designed to be fast-moving, creative and fun, with a strong teaching element.

Holiday clubs are special times. Children can meet with the living God and have great fun as they do so. I challenge you to have as much fun as we did in the preparation and testing of this material!

May you become heroes of faith like Joseph!

Dave Godfrey

Dave Godfrey, March 2005

Dave is an experienced primary teacher, children's worker and numeracy consultant. He leads a weekly outreach children's club in York on behalf of his church. He leads bi-monthly city-wide Praise Parties and an extensive training programme on behalf of the York Schools and Youth Trust. Dave now travels across the UK under the banner of Omega Zone Ministries to train those who work with children, and to lead Praise Party events for children. Dave is a Spring Harvest 8 to 11s leader, and songwriter. He also leads teacher-training events and presents his unique Number Fun numeracy songs in schools across the country.

He has recorded the following CDs of his own Christian children's music:

Brave and Daring	CD/Tape/Songbook
Shoulders of Giants	CD/Songbook &CD/Full Teachers Pack
Heaven's No 1	CD/Tape/Songbook
Dependence Day	CD/Tape
Holy Washing Machine	CD (This CD contains an alternative Joseph theme song called 'Brother Joe'. Visit Dave's website for a soundtrack sample.)

For further information on Dave's ministry, or to order any of his music, contact Dave at dave@omegazone.org.uk
Omega Zone Website: www.omegazone.org.uk

CONTENTS

INTRODUCTION 9
   PYRAMID ROCK terminology

PART 1
WHAT IS PYRAMID ROCK? .. 11
   The aims of **PYRAMID ROCK**
   Theme and setting
   The teaching programme 11
      Day by day
      A sample programme
   Programme breakdown 14

PART 2
SETTING UP A
HOLIDAY CLUB 17
   Big issues 17
      Aims
      Core team
      The children
      Dates and duration
      Team members
   Child protection 19
      Key issues
      Appointing team members
      Training team members
   Venue 21
   Setting up the room
   Finances 22

PART 3
AREAS OF
RESPONSIBILITY 23
   The different jobs and teams needed

PART 4
TRAINING SESSIONS 26
   Session 1 26
   Session 2 29
      Including: Sharing your faith with children
      Working with children with special needs
      Working with children from other faiths

PART 5
RESOURCE BANK 33
   Memory verse 33
   'Pyramid Rock' – theme song 34
   The Adventures of Dr Potty (drama scripts) 36
   Photocopiable forms and artwork 48

PART 6
IDEAS BANK 54
   Up the nile! 54
      Egyptian games
      Egyptian crafts
      Fun Egyptian facts

PART 7
SESSION OUTLINES 57
   Sunday 1 – family service outline 58
   Day 1 – PLANNER 60
   Day 2 – HELPER 66
   Day 3 – PROVIDER 72
   Day 4 – FORGIVER 78
   Day 5 – KING 84
   Sunday 2 – family service outline 90

PART 8:
OTHER WAYS TO USE
PYRAMID ROCK 92
   Follow-up ideas 92
      Eye level clubs
      Adapting **PYRAMID ROCK**
      Other ideas

INTRODUCTION

Joseph is a man who has inspired people down the ages. Despite being mistreated, betrayed and falsely accused, Joseph loved God and maintained his integrity. Children and adults alike can learn from this amazing man!

PYRAMID ROCK is a five-day children's holiday club that focuses on the story, character and experiences of Joseph. It is packed with creative teaching, games, songs, prayers, craft, Bible reading and small-group ideas, along with a drama script for each day.

PYRAMID ROCK provides a mixture of small-group activities and up-front presentation. The material includes two family services – one designed to launch the holiday club and the other to round it off. Alternatively, these could be used to extend the programme to seven days.

Additional resources are:
PYRAMID ROCK DVD This includes the film episode for each day, the **PYRAMID ROCK** song, the memory verse song, backing tracks and training material on how to share your faith with children. Extra artwork is also included. The film is the Joseph episode from  the Testament series, which was produced by S4C and distributed by Bible Society. It has been broken into five chapters, to be used one each day.

JOSEPH'S JOTTER A 48-page booklet containing key passages of the Joseph story from Genesis along with extra information, puzzles and material to use in the  small-group times. This is ideal for use with 8 to 11s.

Pyramid Sheets for under-8s are available in this resource book. Use these in the small group sessions and to take home. Both **JOSEPH'S JOTTER** and the Pyramid Sheets will help maintain contact with children's homes and act as a reminder, in the weeks after the club, of what the children experienced at **PYRAMID ROCK**.

More information on these resources can be found on the inside front cover. The five take-home Pyramid Pieces mentioned at the end of each session have been produced by CPO. For details of all the resources produced by CPO, see the inside back cover.

PYRAMID ROCK TERMINOLOGY

THE HOLIDAY CLUB LEADER The main presenter of the **PYRAMID ROCK** holiday club
THE COOL CATS The music group
PYRAMID GROUPS The small groups that the children will be part of
PYRAMID LEADER Leader of a Pyramid Group
PYRAMID PADS Where Pyramid Groups meet
BOUNCING BENJAMIN Aerobics leader
JOSEPH MEGA-GAME Short interactive screen-based game
UP THE NILE! Refreshment time, Bible reading and listening, games and craft
CAPTAIN KETCHUP A superhero puppet (or a leader dressed up as one) who helps the children 'ketch-up' on the news each day and later presents the children's jokes and contributions which have been put in his special bin.

PART 1
WHAT IS PYRAMID ROCK?

THE AIMS OF PYRAMID ROCK

PYRAMID ROCK is based around the story of Joseph.

> **PYRAMID ROCK** will:
> ▲ introduce the children to a loving God through the stories and experiences of Joseph;
> ▲ encourage the children to put their faith in a faithful God, as Joseph did;
> ▲ hear how Joseph's experiences of God are also the experiences of Pyramid Leaders because of their faith in Jesus Christ;
> ▲ provide a fast-moving, fun and action-packed holiday club programme.

THEME AND SETTING

PYRAMID ROCK is set in 'Ancient Egypt'. Your venue will be transformed into a multicoloured desert paradise, complete with sand, pyramids and other ancient artefacts. The Egyptian theme is picked up in different ways:

▲ Each day, different characters within the story appear to present their side of the story. In doing so, they take us back to ancient Egypt.
▲ The drama for the week is set around the story of Dr Potty and his sister, Princess Potty – a more recent queen of Egypt!
▲ The **PYRAMID ROCK** theme song, Egyptian games and activities.

The **PYRAMID ROCK DVD** tells the story of Joseph in five instalments, using the Testament series produced by S4C and shown on BBC2. In using the material you will probably want to welcome a 'live' Bible character to tell their story and then reinforce this by showing the version of the narrative as told on the DVD. For children already familiar with the Joseph story, the DVD version will bring each incident alive. The story is followed up by group activities.

THE TEACHING PROGRAMME

Joseph was an incredible man who was brought up in a large family, full of intrigue and deception. As a child, his father would have introduced him to the God of his fathers, Abraham and Isaac, much as we will be introducing the children to the same living God. Joseph didn't ask to be the favourite son, or to receive the special multicoloured coat from his father, but both became focal points for his brothers' jealousy. In his immaturity, he openly shared his God-given dreams with his brothers. Even in his youth God showed him the future. In many ways Joseph was on a roller-coaster for the first half of his life. Yet every step of the way he maintained his integrity, faith and love for God – and God used him to bring salvation to the nations, in a thrilling climax to the story.

During this week we'll follow the ups and downs of Joseph's life. The story of Joseph starts in Genesis 37 and ends in chapter 50 – more space is devoted to telling the story of Joseph than those of Adam, Noah or Abraham! Therefore, to avoid story overload, a particular passage has been highlighted for each day. To assist the children in grasping the themes for each day, a key word has been chosen, which will become the focal point of the teaching for each day. The most important section of **PYRAMID ROCK** is the teaching programme, which should be well planned, prayed through, prepared and presented clearly. The programme will challenge the children to follow the Lord just as Joseph did years ago.

DAY BY DAY

SUNDAY 1: A GREAT BIG GOD WITH A GREAT BIG PROMISE
KEY STORY: The promise of God to Abraham
KEY LINK TO THE HOLIDAY CLUB: This story is the background to the story of Joseph. Abraham is Joseph's great-grandfather, and Joseph becomes a major player in the fulfilment of this amazing promise.
KEY PASSAGE: Genesis 12:1–5

DAY 1: PLANNER
KEY BELIEF: The loving God had a plan for Joseph and his brothers, just as he has plans for us.
KEY STORY: Introducing the sons of Jacob and telling the story of how Joseph was sold into slavery.
KEY PASSAGE: Genesis 37

DAY 2: HELPER
KEY BELIEF: God is our helper – he is always with us and gives us strength and wisdom.
KEY STORY: Joseph's life in Egypt – in the house of Potiphar and in prison.
KEY PASSAGE: Genesis 39,40

DAY 3: PROVIDER
KEY BELIEF: God provides for his people. He provided favour, food, wisdom and dreams for Joseph.
KEY STORY: Joseph interprets the dreams of Pharaoh and provides food for the nations.
KEY PASSAGE: Genesis 41

DAY 4: FORGIVER
KEY BELIEF: God loves to forgive! Joseph was like his God, and showed forgiveness to those who had hurt him.
KEY STORY: Joseph's brothers come to Egypt for food, and Joseph forgives his repentant brothers.
KEY PASSAGE: Genesis 42:1 – 45:24

DAY 5: KING
KEY BELIEF: God is in control of the nations. He is powerful and good.
KEY STORY: Joseph and his family are reunited again. Joseph looks back on his life and sees God at work. Joseph acknowledges that he was in Egypt 'for such a time as this'.
KEY PASSAGES: Genesis 45:25 – 47:12

SUNDAY 2 – FORGIVENESS IS FOREVER!
KEY STORY: Joseph tells his brothers that his forgiveness is sincere.
KEY LINK TO THE HOLIDAY CLUB: Summarising the teaching from the week and clearly stating that God's forgiveness, like Joseph's, lasts forever!
KEY PASSAGE: Genesis 50:15–26

HELPFUL SYMBOLS
Throughout the book, you will see these two symbols:

ALL TOGETHER
Whenever you see this logo, it means that all the children are together to do these activities.

PYRAMID GROUPS
This logo indicates that these activities are to be done in Pyramid Groups, in each group's Pyramid Pad.

A SAMPLE PROGRAMME

This suggested programme takes two and a quarter hours, but the material can be adapted to take up more or less time.

You may not have time to do all the activities in the programme, so choose those activities which best suit your club.

EVENT	RUNNING TIME	INCLUDES
TEAM PREPARATION AND PRAYER	30 minutes	Spiritual and practical preparation
PYRAMID GROUP WELCOME	10 minutes	Time in Pyramid Groups
RED HOT!	40 minutes	Key word Bouncing Benjamin Joseph mega-game **PYRAMID ROCK** theme song Red Hot News – with Captain Ketchup **PYRAMID ROCK DVD** and/or key witness
UP THE NILE!	40 minutes	At the oasis – refreshment time Open the scrolls – Bible exploration Egyptian games and craft activities
PYRAMID ROCKS!	40 minutes	Mega Question Testimony - focusing on the day's teaching Songs Captain Ketchup's bin Memory jogger (and memory verse song) Drama for the day Creative prayer Theme song
PYRAMID GROUPS	5 minutes	The children collect their belongings (and a Pyramid Piece), and depart.
TEAM TIME	45 minutes	Tidying up, team debrief and preparation for the following day.

PROGRAMME BREAKDOWN

Each day's programme contains the following elements:

TEAM PREPARATION

AIMS
The main aims for the day, with some ideas to help you think about how the children will engage with the theme on each day.

TEAM PREPARATION
Notes to help you prepare for the day, including:
▲ Bible reading and study – to ensure that the team members are familiar with the themes and teaching for the day, and provide a chance for the team to study the Bible for themselves, in a devotional way.
▲ Prayer.
▲ Final encouragements and practical issues.

EQUIPMENT CHECKLIST
A useful way of checking that all the resources are ready for the day.

PYRAMID GROUP WELCOME
When the children arrive at **PYRAMID ROCK**, they will register and go straight into their Pyramid Groups. During this group time, the key aims will be team-building, getting-to-know-you and feedback. On days 2 to 5, this is an excellent opportunity for Pyramid Leaders to ask the children if they can remember the memory verse and the key words for each day. This ten-minute section allows late arrivals to join the group before RED HOT! Any children bringing pictures or jokes for Captain Ketchup should be encouraged to put them in Captain Ketchup's bin as they arrive.

RED HOT!
This section of the programme is designed to be fast moving and fun. It contains the main teaching for the day and other elements outlined below. During this period of time, the children are all together for activities led from the front.

KEY WORD
The key word for the day is introduced at the start of the programme. As well as setting the theme for the day, it will help children link the various sections of the programme together in their minds.

BOUNCING BENJAMIN
This is an aerobic workout, giving the children a chance to stretch their muscles in a fun way. It can include simple exercises, but it can be made exciting by using fun actions which fit in with the Egyptian or teaching themes. This should be set to fast, lively music. Be aware of any children with disabilities – if you have a child in a wheelchair, for example, include lots of hand actions.

JOSEPH MEGA-GAME
This is a short team game, best played in Pyramid Groups. Children are shown a slide on the screen, and set a challenge to complete in a short amount of time. The game is generally theme-related and you will find a set of prepared pictures for each day to photocopy at the end of each day's outline. Due to the high-speed nature of these short games, it usually works best if the children call out the answers and their Pyramid Leader takes notes. The Holiday Club Leader then quickly reveals the answers to the challenge, with the Pyramid Leaders marking their team's sheet. Declare the team with the most correct answers 'Joseph mega-game champions' for the day. You could run a points system during your week and award points for the winning team. See the **PYRAMID ROCK** website for ideas about using a points system through the week.

THE COOL CATS
Children enjoy singing and learning new songs. Choose a small selection of songs, including the **PYRAMID ROCK** song, so that the children can become familiar with them.

RED HOT NEWS WITH CAPTAIN KETCHUP
The teaching elements are introduced by Red Hot News, read by Captain Ketchup from a prepared script. Captain Ketchup can either be a person live on stage, or a puppet presenting from behind a puppet screen. This superhero's job is to help the children 'ketch-up' on the previous day's storyline, and to pose an intriguing thought or two about where the story will go from here. This section should either be presented visually with simple drawings on the OHP or PowerPoint, or a mixture of pictures and artefacts. Use your imagination and ingenuity to make this section work. Some suitable artwork is available in *How to cheat at visual aids* (SU, £9.99, 1 85999 500 4).

Captain Ketchup puppets are available by special request from One Way UK (0845 490 1930 or www.onewayuk.com). If the character is played by an adult, then they should wear as much red as possible, including a big red cape. Red Hot News merges with the Joseph story for each day, either told with the DVD or by the key witness. Captain Ketchup initially comes out of news reading mode and interacts with the key witness.

Each day, when Captain Ketchup arrives, the whole club should do the Captain Ketchup dance! Make up a short, easy-to-learn dance to music and teach it the other children on the first day of your club. Download the music used in the **PYRAMID ROCK** trial from the Omega Zone website (see page 6).

THE KEY WITNESS

The key witness is one of the characters from the story, who relates what has happened to the children. The witness should be played by a confident actor who has learnt the script before the session, adding as much emotion and feeling as possible to their storytelling. They should come to the front dressed appropriately. This will really help the children to engage in the story. If you are using the **PYRAMID ROCK DVD**, look for ways to link Captain Ketchup's news with the day's episode.

THE PYRAMID ROCK DVD

The five chapters of this DVD provide a small part of the Joseph story each day in a different medium. You may choose to tell the story first and then show the DVD to reinforce the storyline. Children learn in a variety of ways and this will help them learn in the way most appropriate for them. Alternatively, you may choose to just show the DVD and follow it up with questions to ensure the children have grasped the story.

UP THE NILE!

A time in Pyramid Groups, which will help children and team members build relationships as they have refreshments and explore the Bible together.

AT THE OASIS

Be creative in providing refreshments. Try making shaped biscuits (pyramids, sphinx, mummies etc) or multicoloured cakes. This section should allow the children to have a drink and go to the toilet. Remember to provide for children with food allergies and look out for issues of health and safety.

OPEN THE SCROLLS

It is vitally important to help children read the Bible for themselves, or listen to it being read. The time together when you engage with God's Word is a central part of the programme. *Joseph's Jotter* and the Pyramid Sheets provide a structure for doing this, and suggestions are given to help group discussion. Adapt the questions that are given according to the personality of the leader and the nature of the group. If you are using Bibles instead of *Joseph's Jotter*, make sure that the verses are in a child-accessible version and easy to read. You may want to copy the most relevant verses onto an acetate or sheets of paper, so that the children can see them clearly.

EGYPTIAN GAMES AND CRAFT

Theme games and craft activities exploring the theme. These can be done in Pyramid Groups or larger groups. See the Ideas bank on page 54 for loads of creative ideas.

PYRAMID ROCKS!

During this section of the programme the children are all together for activities led from the front.

MEGA QUESTION

As the different groups return from their various activities, display a key question that focuses the children's thoughts back to the main teaching point of the day. This should initially be discussed within groups, before the Holiday Club Leader takes a few answers from the children or team members. They then remind everyone of the main teaching point made earlier in the day.

TESTIMONY

Due to the fact that the entire holiday club focuses on an Old Testament story, God the Father is prominent. Leaders will also want to introduce children to God the Son. Testimony is the best way to share something about what a relationship with Jesus means in reality. This is so important that a training feature has been included in the **PYRAMID ROCK DVD**. Make the training for this a priority in your preparation for the club. One leader, child or guest should be asked to prepare a short testimony each day that focuses on the theme for the day, preferably with the use of visual aids. The testimony could be given in an interview style or as a straight talk. This is the opportunity to share how someone can become a Christian (particularly on Day 4).

MEMORY JOGGER

From the front, review the story of the day, including the key word. This is the time to include memory verse activities. See page 33 for some creative ideas on how to use memory verses, including information on the memory verse song for the week. The memory verse is from Stephen's speech to the Sanhedrin in Acts 7:9,10. It reflects the important place Joseph holds in the history of God's people. God was with him in all his troubles!

CAPTAIN KETCHUP'S BIN

Captain Ketchup reappears to read out some of the jokes and show some of the pictures children have brought to the club and put in his dustbin. If your Captain Ketchup is a puppet, then the Holiday Club Leader or an alternative 'glamorous assistant' will need to help him with his post!

'THE ADVENTURES OF DR POTTY' DRAMA

You will follow the story of Dr Potty and his niece, Denise, as they go in search of the onion-shaped piece that is missing from the 'Relic with the Missing Onion Shaped Piece'! Each story links to the key word for the day.

CREATIVE PRAYER

At the end of each session outline is a creative prayer idea, which everyone can take part in and enjoy.

THEME SONG

It's always good to finish with a song. This could be the **PYRAMID ROCK** theme song, which you will find on pages 34 and 35. Full and backing track recordings can be found on the accompanying DVD.

PYRAMID GROUPS

Each day the children can be given a take-home Pyramid Piece, available from CPO (see the inside back cover for details). By the end of Day 5, the children will have the five pieces they need to complete their pyramid. A great way of encouraging the children and their families to come to the family service or party at the end of the week is to ask the children to cut out and construct their pyramids and to bring them back for presentation at the family service or party.

TEAM TIME

This is time to clear up, prepare for the next session, pray together and even have a meal together. Do ensure that you make time to review the session that has just passed. The evaluation form on page 50 will help you do this.

PART 2
SETTING UP A HOLIDAY CLUB

This section of the material will help you to think through the issues that need to be addressed in order to set up a **PYRAMID ROCK** holiday club.

BIG ISSUES

▲ What are the specific aims of running your holiday club?
▲ Is the holiday club part of the ongoing outreach or strategy for the children and youth work of your church? If not, how does it fit in?
▲ Will the holiday club have the prayer support and financial support of your church?
▲ Do you have the people needed to make **PYRAMID ROCK** a reality?
▲ Is there a wider vision for reaching the families of the children you are hoping will come to the club? If so, how can you make the most of the holiday club week? (See Part 8.)
▲ How will you follow up your link with those children and families you have had contact with in the week? (See Part 8.)

AIMS

Each holiday club will have specific aims. A programme such as **PYRAMID ROCK** can provide a manageable, creative and fun way of reaching out to the children of your neighbourhood with the good news of Jesus. A holiday club can provide an excellent opportunity to blow any misconceptions away and to reveal to children with no church connection a God who loves them passionately.

The broad aims of **PYRAMID ROCK**, as outlined in Part 1, are to:
▲ introduce the children to a loving God through the stories and experiences of Joseph;
▲ hear how Joseph's experiences of God are also the experiences of Pyramid Leaders through their faith in Jesus Christ;
▲ encourage the children to put their faith in a faithful God, as Joseph did;
▲ provide a fast-moving, fun and action-packed holiday club programme.

Alongside these broad aims, you may have some more specific aims. For example:
▲ to attract new children to join your church's Sunday groups or other children's activities;
▲ to develop your team members' gifts and experience;
▲ to present the gospel to children who've never heard it;
▲ to provide an opportunity for children to make an initial or further commitment to follow Jesus;
▲ to get to know the children in your church;
▲ to provide a project to encourage your church to work together;
▲ to establish links with the children's families;
▲ to encourage cooperation with other churches or groups in your area;
▲ to launch an ongoing children's group based on the **PYRAMID ROCK** theme;
▲ to give parents a few mornings off during the school holidays;
▲ to develop your families' ministry.

Any or all of these aims may be appropriate, but you'll have to decide what you want to achieve in your situation with **PYRAMID ROCK**. If you have several aims, you'll need to decide which are the most important. You'll also need to evaluate **PYRAMID ROCK** afterwards, to see if you met your aims. Decide now how you'll do that. How will you measure success?

CORE TEAM

All the helpers should be involved in planning and preparing for **PYRAMID ROCK**, but you will need a smaller team to coordinate things and make some initial decisions. As well as the holiday club's overall leader, this should include your most experienced team members, your minister and your children's workers.

There are a number of legal duties placed upon those who run holiday clubs. This will vary even within the UK. You will need to check with your own Social and Education Services with regard to current legislation.

THE CHILDREN

Having set your aims, you'll be able to make other key decisions, such as:

- ▲ Who will you invite to **PYRAMID ROCK**?
- ▲ Do your aims relate primarily to the children already involved in your church, or those outside it?
- ▲ How many children do you want to involve? If your main aim is to get to know the children better, you might need to restrict numbers. On the other hand, if you want to present the gospel to children who haven't heard it, you may want as many as possible to attend.
- ▲ What age range(s) do you want to target with **PYRAMID ROCK**? Do you want to cater for an age range that is well represented in your groups, or one that isn't? Will you be able to tailor the activities in a way that will appeal to a wide age range? **PYRAMID ROCK** is designed for use with children between the ages of 5 and 11. You will find some thoughts about using the material with other age ranges in Part 8, on page 92.

DATES AND DURATION

You'll need to fix the date for your holiday club early enough for people to take it into account when they book their holidays. It is also essential that the dates do not clash with other holiday clubs in the area, activities already booked at your premises, holidays organised by local schools, holidays or camps for local Boys' or Girls' Brigade, Cub or Brownie groups, and carnivals or local events taking place in your area.

The potential team members' availability will have the most effect on the duration of your holiday club. If most of your team need to take time off work, it may not be practical to run a full five-day club.

Whatever your plans, it is good practice to inform OFSTED, in writing, of your **PYRAMID ROCK** club. However, you must by law register **PYRAMID ROCK** if you are meeting for more than two hours a day, for more than six days in the year. Remember that other follow-up events may take you over your total of six days. If your event does not exceed this limit, but you have under-8s in your group, it is good practice still to inform OFSTED. If in doubt, phone OFSTED and check with the Local Day Care Advisor – he or she is there to help!

Of course, there are many ways to use **PYRAMID ROCK** – perhaps as an after-school club, Saturday club or a Sunday teaching programme. Part 8 gives some ideas for adapting **PYRAMID ROCK**.

TEAM MEMBERS

There are many different roles for team members in **PYRAMID ROCK** (see page 23). It's important to note that your team members do not all have to be experienced children's workers. Many people in your church will be quite capable of leading or helping a small group of children after some initial basic training; and others will be suitable for other roles, such as musicians, registrars and caterers. Of course, many of the team members with these supporting roles may be Pyramid Leaders as well. The table below shows the minimum recommended adult-to-child ratios.

ADULT-TO-CHILD RATIOS

The recommended adult to child ratios are as follows:

0 to 2 years – one adult to every three children (1:3)
2 to 3 years – one adult to every four children (1:4)
3 to 8 years – one adult to every eight children (1:8)
over-8s – one adult for the first eight children, followed by one for every 12 (1:12).

There should always be more than one adult for any group and at least one should be female.

PYRAMID ROCK is an ideal opportunity to develop and nurture the gifts and experience of the young people in your church, in a structured and supervised environment. Bear in mind, though, that for the purpose of child protection matters, a child is defined as being under 18. In other words, if you have a number of helpers under the age of 18, you will need more adult team members, not less.

At first sight this may seem strange, because young team members can be extremely helpful and competent, and can therefore make the adult team member's job much easier. But it makes sense if we understand that even the most competent helpers will need to be mentored and encouraged if their gifts are to be developed to their full potential. Avoid the temptation of only giving your younger helpers the mundane or less challenging tasks. If you are aiming to stretch your helpers, then they will need the help and support of an adult team member.

CHILD PROTECTION
KEY ISSUES

The welfare of the children we hope to reach through **PYRAMID ROCK** is of paramount importance. We are concerned for their spiritual welfare, but also, of course, for their physical and emotional welfare. Sadly, nowadays children are at risk as much as ever before, and it is our duty to do all we can to ensure their safety and well-being as we aim to show them God's love.

All churches should have a clear child protection policy. If you have an established procedure for your church, all of the holiday club team must go through that process. If you don't have a procedure in place, a special club week is a good opportunity to establish one. The following notes outline the main issues.

ENGLAND AND WALES

Following the coming into law of the Children Act, the government published a code of practice for groups working with children called *Safe from Harm*, which contains a number of guidelines for good practice. Most denominations now have established good practice policies based on this and it is important that you work according to the one that applies to you. For further advice or information in the UK, contact the Churches' Child Protection Advisory Service (CCPAS) on 0845 120 4550.

Safe from Harm contains guidelines rather than law, but you need to show that you have taken them into consideration. In fact, if you ignore such good practice your insurance may be invalid.

One important action is to ensure all those with access to children under 18 (volunteers or in paid employment) make a signed declaration of any criminal conviction, including those 'spent' under the Rehabilitation of Offenders Act 1974, along with details of cautions, reprimands or warnings. Your denomination will probably require you to make use of the Criminal Records Bureau. CCPAS can advise you on this too.

SCOTLAND

If you are using **PYRAMID ROCK** in Scotland, you should seek advice from your local social work office about registering the group. Most social work offices have a community worker employed with them and they are always helpful when it comes to advice about legislation and procedures. With regard to younger children it would always be sensible to seek advice and guidance from the Care Commission, who are a national organisation.

Most denominations now have established good-practice policies and guidelines, and it is important that you work according to the one that applies to you. The Protection of Children in Scotland Act (2003) states that anyone working in a 'child care' position must be checked by Disclosure Scotland as part of the recruitment process before they can begin their appointment. Voluntary organisations can register with the Central Registered Body in Scotland (CRBS) to gain access to free checks. Contact the CRBS on 01786 849777 or Disclosure Scotland on 0870 6096006. CCPAS can also advise you.

NORTHERN IRELAND

If you are using **PYRAMID ROCK** in Northern Ireland, you should seek advice from your local DHSS about registering the group. Most Social Services offices will have a Social Services Early Years Team. They will help with advice about legislation and procedures. The Early Years Teams have a statutory responsibility for the registration and inspection of all day care services for children from birth to 12 years under the Children (NI) Order 1995.

Most denominations now have established good-practice policies and guidelines based on 'Our Duty to Care', and 'Getting it right – standards of good practice for child protection' and it is important that you work according to these. Churches in Northern Ireland can obtain information on the suitability of workers (whether paid or voluntary) by obtaining a POCVA (Protection of Children and Vulnerable Adults) List check. Contact the Child Care Unit of the DHSSPS on 028 9052 2559. Details of 'Getting it right' can be obtained from the Volunteer Development Agency on 028 9023 6100.

APPOINTING TEAM MEMBERS

Failure to take the necessary steps could lead to a claim of negligence against the church if a child comes to any harm at the hands of anyone working with them in a voluntary capacity. 'Harm' includes ill-treatment of any kind (including sexual abuse) or impairment of physical or mental health or development.

You should ask all potential team members to sign a form such as the one below. Emphasise that it represents positive action for good practice, and does not imply any slur or suspicion. Obviously, the nature of the form is sensitive and should be handled with care. Ensure that confidentiality is maintained. In accordance with the Data Protection Act, do not divulge any information to third parties.

If anyone gives a 'yes' answer, allow the individual to explain this disclosure personally or by letter. If you are in any doubt about the person's suitability, consult your church leader.

CONFIDENTIAL DECLARATION FOR POTENTIAL TEAM MEMBERS

Guidelines from the Home Office following the Children Act 1989 advise that all voluntary organisations, including churches, take steps to safeguard the children who are entrusted to their care. You are therefore asked to make the following declarations:

Because of the nature of the work for which you are applying, this post is exempt from the provision of Section 4(ii) of the Rehabilitation of Offenders Act 1974, by virtue of the Rehabilitation of Offenders Act 1974 (Exemptions) Order 1975, and you are therefore not entitled to withhold information about convictions which, for other purposes are 'spent' under the provisions of the Act. In the event of an appointment, any failure to disclose such convictions could result in the withdrawal of approval to work with children in the church.

Do you have any current or spent criminal convictions, cautions, bindovers or cases pending?

YES ☐   NO ☐

Has anyone ever expressed concern about the safety of children in your care?

YES ☐   NO ☐

SIGNED   **DATE**

As well as the declaration form, it is recommended that potential team members offer one name as a referee. Questions to ask a referee might include:
▲ In what capacity have you known the applicant, and for how long?
▲ How willing and able are they to work with others?
▲ How suitable would you consider them for work with children and young people?
▲ Are there any relevant details about this applicant which cause you concern?

Do not allow people who have not been through your process to have unsupervised access to children.

TRAINING TEAM MEMBERS

Undertaking some basic skills and knowledge training is vital for the success of the holiday club. You should aim to have at least two sessions together in preparation, and you should ensure that these are more or less compulsory for team members. As part of these sessions, the vision and practicalities of **PYRAMID ROCK** can also be outlined.

In Part 4, you will find a training outline for two training/preparation sessions.

VENUE

Choosing a venue is a very important issue. Sometimes a community hall or school is a well-equipped, neutral venue that can be non-threatening for children and parents outside the church. However, you may wish to use this opportunity to introduce the children and parents to your church building. This can also help save on the cost of hiring an alternative venue. The venue does need to have enough space for the number of children and the type of activities you are planning. You will need access to the venue before the holiday club to ensure the necessary preparations can be made.

Even if you don't need to register your holiday club under the Children Act, carefully consider the following requirements laid down by the Act as sensible guidelines to be interpreted with common sense. If you must register, you won't have any choice!

Requirements for accommodation state that the premises should be warm, clean and adequately lit and ventilated, with clearly marked emergency exits. The minimum unencumbered floor space to be provided for children aged 5 to 8 years is 25 square feet (2.3 square metres) per child. In other words, be careful about very large numbers of children in a small hall, and work out the maximum number of children who can attend.

It is worth doing a risk assessment of the premises a few weeks before the club starts. The premises should meet Health and Safety requirements. Check that the owners have complied with all the requirements, including the provision of adequate insurance, for the purpose of the holiday club. Ideally there should be one toilet and one hand basin for every ten children. Disposable towels or hot-air hand driers are preferable to roller towels. If you are preparing food on site, you will need to be inspected by the Environmental Health Officer. The person with overall responsibility for the catering arrangements should have the minimum of the Basic Food and Hygiene Certificate. Smoking should not be permitted on the premises. Children should not be allowed unsupervised access to the kitchen.

SETTING UP THE ROOM

The holiday club will be greatly enhanced if the main room you are using is transformed into a multicoloured Egyptian paradise! This will help create a wonderful atmosphere and spark the children's imagination. You will need to think creatively about how you can transform your venue. The creative use of cardboard, wood, paint and other materials can make a real difference. Think creatively about what you can hang from the ceiling, cover the walls with and put on the floor. You may wish to create a giant version of the pyramid on the Pyramid Pieces!

To transform the area you could:
▲ Cover the walls with big pictures of pyramids (each small group could have a massive pyramid in their team colour next to their Pyramid Pad);
▲ Create a background of palm trees, camels and something of a desert flavour;
▲ Make a puppet screen out of black material with a sandy coloured pyramid and camels sewn onto it;
▲ Serve refreshments from the mouth of the sphinx!
▲ Decorate the hall with multicoloured drapes, parachutes etc;
▲ Have registration take place under a multicoloured umbrella, using canvas chairs or deckchairs.

THE STAGE AREA

You will need a focal point at the front from which the Holiday Club Leader can run the programme. Create a Red Hot News area on one side of the stage. Think about where you will do your dramas and where the band will be positioned. You will also need to decide where the OHP/projector screen should be located. A draped-off area or an attached room needs to be provided for the entrance of the actors in the drama. Alternatively they could appear from behind Captain Ketchup's puppet screen. The boundary for the stage area could be marked by a masking tape line across the floor.

PYRAMID PADS

The rest of the room can be split up into Pyramid Pads, in which the Pyramid Groups are located. Colour-coded pyramids could be created to highlight the location of the groups. Keep chairs out of the way, except for those who cannot sit on the floor, so that the room can be used for the energetic sections of the programme without objects getting in the way.

FINANCES

You'll need to consider your financial resources. Work out what you'll need money for. Examples might include:

▲ craft materials;
▲ refreshments;
▲ materials for the scenery;
▲ photocopying/printing costs;
▲ hire of premises;
▲ hire of equipment such as video projector;
▲ **PYRAMID ROCK** books for your team members;
▲ resources such as the **PYRAMID ROCK DVD**, Pyramid Sheets and *Joseph's Jotters*;
▲ prizes or presents for the children (see the 'Points system' article on the **PYRAMID ROCK** website).

Do you need to do some fund-raising? Will you charge a small fee for children to attend **PYRAMID ROCK**? Does the church allocate money within the budget for holiday club, seeing it as a significant investment?

PART 3
AREAS OF RESPONSIBILITY

A successful holiday club requires a variety of support teams to be set up and individuals to take responsibility for different areas of the programme. Listed below are the different teams you will need and the key roles people will need to assume before, during and after the event. Some people will be able to play more than one role in **PYRAMID ROCK**.

DRAMA TEAM

A small team of five people should take responsibility for the **PYRAMID ROCK** drama. These people need to be reasonably confident, able to project their voices and to act both 'big' and silly! They should be willing to learn their lines and to practise each sketch until they can perform it with confidence. These sketches work especially well if you can find a young person to play the part of Denise.

One of the drama team (or another person) needs to take the role of Props Manager, and collect and prepare all the props.

HOLIDAY CLUB LEADER/ PRESENTATION TEAM

The Holiday Club Leader coordinates the upfront leading of the club. They will usually be the overall leader of the club, but this does not need to be the case. You will also need to find someone to lead the following parts of the programme:
▲ Captain Ketchup
▲ Bouncing Benjamin

The quality of presentation speaks volumes about the quality of your holiday club, so make sure your visuals are in focus, clearly written (ideally computer generated), in a legible child-friendly font and big enough for the children who are furthest away from the screen to see.

MUSICAL TEAM – THE COOL CATS

If you can't use live music, sing along to a CD player. If you do have a live band, ask the musicians to dress up in outrageously multicoloured clothes! Cats were sacred animals to the Ancient Egyptians. Why not give the band some cat hats to wear? Alternatively you could invite the children to choose a name for the band on the first day.

PRINTING AND PUBLICITY

A small team, including at least one computer literate person, should take responsibility for all the design, printing and publicity for **PYRAMID ROCK**. Your aim should be to produce publicity that is visually impressive, consistent, accurate and attractive.

The publicity will need to be colourful, and use the **PYRAMID ROCK** logo (either photocopied from this book or downloaded from the website), a child-friendly font and suitable pictures.

The publicity team should take responsibility for:
▲ posters and fliers to advertise **PYRAMID ROCK**;
▲ a registration form for each child (see sample version on page 48);
▲ a consent form for parents/guardians/carers (see sample version on page 48);
▲ an invitation card or letter to go with the appropriate forms;
▲ helpers' forms for potential team members to indicate the roles they'd like to do – this could include the declaration form on page 20;
▲ helper's notes and training materials. Even if someone else writes this material, the printing and publicity team should be responsible for the layout;

- ▲ name badges for the team leaders and for any adults who are on site and part of **PYRAMID ROCK**;
- ▲ signs and notices. These will be needed around the site, including the main hall, entrances, toilets and areas that are out of bounds. These should use the same typeface and colours as other materials to maintain the consistent **PYRAMID ROCK** scheme;
- ▲ prayer cards/bookmarks – prayer pointers to help church members to pray for the holiday club before, during and after **PYRAMID ROCK** events.

See page 48 for sample **PYRAMID ROCK** registration and consent forms.

CPO produces a wide range of **PYRAMID ROCK** publicity and other merchandise. For details, see the inside back cover.

REFRESHMENT TEAM

This team will play a vital role during the week. They will be responsible for:
- ▲ checking with the registration team that you have no children with food allergies;
- ▲ obtaining and preparing the refreshments for the children;
- ▲ tidying up after the refreshments have been given out.

For this team to work efficiently you may like to choose one person to coordinate the group. At least one person on this team should have the Basic Food Hygiene certificate. Think about using disposable cups or bottles to save on washing-up time.

Some holiday club teams have lunch together after each session – a good chance to unwind and debrief, and have fun together!

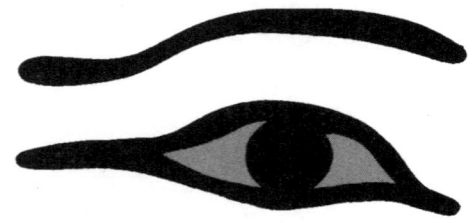

REGISTRATION TEAM

This team will be responsible for ensuring that the wording on the registration form is correct, welcoming everyone and registering the children when they arrive.

SECURITY PERSON

The person in charge of security will be responsible for ensuring that no child leaves the building unless they have permission to do so, and that only children or adults who are part of **PYRAMID ROCK** are allowed to enter the building.

It is important for each adult to have an appropriate, clearly labelled badge to identify them and their role. The children registered for **PYRAMID ROCK** should have their own badge. Any adult or child on site not wearing an appropriate badge should be challenged.

If you are running a large holiday club, or if you are inviting a number of children who have no other contact with your church, it can be difficult to know whether the person collecting a child is the one who is authorised to do so. In such a situation, a form of 'receipt' slip is useful (see page 49).

If, when dropping off the child, the parent signs the reverse to say that their child may go home alone or with someone else, the registrar should give that slip to the child's **PYRAMID LEADER** during the session.

If a person wants to collect a child, but neither they nor the Pyramid Leader has the slip, they should be referred to the overall leader, who will ensure they are authorised to collect the child.

PYRAMID LEADERS AND ASSISTANTS

The Pyramid Leader's role is to get to know the children so that they feel welcome and comfortable at **PYRAMID ROCK**. The programme is designed to give the Pyramid Leaders enough time in their Pyramid Pads to have meaningful discussions, including ones which apply the teaching programme to the children's lives. These leaders are going to show the children what it means in practice to have a relationship with Jesus.

Young or inexperienced team members can be assistant leaders. This helps the group leader, as well as allowing the assistants to develop their own gifts and skills under supervision. Their example can have a powerful effect upon the children.

If you have a large holiday club, you may choose to appoint Pyramid Coordinators to oversee six or eight Pyramid Groups (all in the same age range). It is best if these coordinators do not have a group of their own.

Make sure your team members know that it is not appropriate for them to talk to children alone as this can be misinterpreted. The government has made it clear that actions such as guiding with a hand on the shoulder or comforting a distressed young child would not be considered inappropriate. It is a question of common sense in this area, but if in doubt, don't touch a child! You must have an agreed procedure in the case of a child disclosing abuse, or a situation that puts children at risk. Your church's Child Protection policy should outline a procedure. If not, contact CCPAS (details on page 19).

The Pyramid Leaders have a specific responsibility for the children in their Pyramid Group during the week. They should sit with the children on all occasions, answering their questions and prompting them to discover more about Joseph and about Jesus.

The Pyramid Leaders should all be dressed as if they are in the desert – shorts, T-shirts, sunglasses, hats – anything that suggests hot weather! See the inside back cover for details of **PYRAMID ROCK** T-shirts.

FIRST-AIDER

Appoint at least one member of your team as the official first-aider. If possible appoint assistant first-aiders – a male for the boys and a female for the girls. These people will need a current first-aid certificate, and access to a first-aid kit. You will also need an accident book to record any incidents or accidents. This is essential in the event of any insurance claim. A record of the matter should be noted, along with details of action taken. It should be countersigned where appropriate.

The entire team needs to know who the first-aiders are, any emergency procedures, including fire exits and assembly points, and where to access a telephone in case of emergency.

CRAFT AND EQUIPMENT

Someone should take responsibility for making sure that everything that is needed for the craft, creative prayer and Pyramid Group activities is in the correct place at the right time.

TECHNICAL MANAGER

The amount of technology used will vary with the size and nature of each club. A technical manager could take responsibility for:
▲ balancing the levels on the public address system (this is especially important if you are running various musicians and presenters through the system);
▲ any TV, video, overhead projector or video projection equipment being used.

If you are running a club with less than fifty children, one or two TV sets can be used to show the DVD. To link two sets, you'll need a coaxial cable and a 'splitter', so that the DVD signal can be sent to both TVs. If you have more than fifty children, you should consider using a video projector. Either way, the sound would be better if played through your PA system rather than relying on the TV or projector speakers.

PART 4 TRAINING SESSIONS

You will need to find a couple of suitable evenings or a weekend to put on these sessions. Feel free to adapt them to your needs, but here they are structured for two, two-hour sessions.

SESSION 1
The big picture – leading a small group

INTRODUCTION The basic outline of **PYRAMID ROCK**
SECTION 1 Looking at how God used a young man – to inspire us!
SECTION 2 Leading a small group
SECTION 3 Keeping control of your group

EQUIPMENT Flip chart and pens (or some other way of recording feedback and presenting material), slips of paper with Bible verses for section 1; slips with role-play descriptions for section 2

INTRODUCTION
Talk through the aims of this session together. Give a basic introduction to **PYRAMID ROCK** and the aims behind the holiday club. Discuss any issues that arise.

SECTION 1
Looking at how God used a young man – to inspire us!

Tell the group that you are going to:
▲ look at what the Bible says about the young boy called Joseph;
▲ think about the influences upon Joseph's growing faith;
▲ look at what Jesus said about children and his kingdom.

Split your leaders into small groups. Ask each group to look at the passages below and to think creatively about the issues raised by the following questions:

GENESIS 30:22–24
▲ Why was Joseph such a special boy for Rachel?

GENESIS 35:16–21
▲ Talk about how the death of his mother Rachel in child-birth might have affected the young boy Joseph. Can we see any evidence of this in his later life?

GENESIS 37:1–11
▲ How does Joseph interact with his brothers?
▲ How much does Joseph know about the God of his fathers?

It is impossible to know who played a role in the development of Joseph's faith or how his faith developed. But we do know that by the time he was in Potiphar's house he had made it clear he worshipped the true God and had experienced God in his life (Genesis 39:1–3). What role have we got to play in developing the faith of children who come to **PYRAMID ROCK?**
▲ What might we reasonably expect to be the outcome of our holiday club in the children's lives?
▲ What do you think God might reveal to the children during **PYRAMID ROCK**?
▲ How did the favouritism shown by his father impact the life of young Joseph? How might our behaviour affect the children who come to **PYRAMID ROCK**?
▲ Do you think Joseph could have ended up as Prime Minister of Egypt without being sold by his brothers?

Spend some time reflecting together as a bigger group, recording what you have discussed. The overall leader should help guide the conversation and bring out particular points. Here are a few key thoughts:

▲ Joseph needed introducing to the God of his fathers through Rachel (initially), Jacob and his extended family. At **PYRAMID ROCK** we are helping the children know the same God. It is likely to be part of a long process, which we should encourage the wider church family to engage in.

▲ God had plans for Joseph, even from birth. God has plans and purposes for the children we will meet during **PYRAMID ROCK** (and for the team too!).

▲ Joseph listened to God, and probably communicated openly with him – even though his attitude got him into trouble with his brothers. The children we meet will have diverse backgrounds, attitudes and needs, but each one has the potential of finding their loving God and walking in his ways.

Encourage the team with Jesus' words in Matthew 19:14. Jesus came to bring his people into his kingdom which is for children and for all who are like them. We can go into **PYRAMID ROCK** with real confidence that God loves the children and that he is passionate that they put their faith in him, just like Joseph did.

Thank God for his love of children and the privilege of sharing that love with the children of your area.

SECTION 2
Leading a small group

Leading a small group of children is a vital part of **PYRAMID ROCK**. Pyramid Leaders will be the ones who get to know the children and build relationships with them. Sometimes these relationships can develop into long-term friendships. Understanding how these groups work and having guidelines is really important.

INTRODUCTION TO ROLE-PLAY ACTIVITY
Ask the teams to split into groups of no more than seven, in order to play the roles of a small group of children at **PYRAMID ROCK**. Some team members will be more comfortable with this activity than others, but encourage them all to participate! Tell the team that they are going to have a go at the large sheet of paper activity for Open the scrolls on Day 2.

Firstly outline the activity to the team (see below), then give each member of the group one of the traits listed below on a slip of paper. One is the group leader, and the others represent different children's characters and behaviour. You may need to select the person who plays 'leader' in advance since this is a more challenging role that not everyone would feel able to take on. Tell the team not to show anyone their piece of paper, but to act it out during the activity as best they can. However, make sure the team doesn't totally overact and make their group leader's role a total nightmare! Each group will need a large sheet of paper and pens and should be given ten minutes for the task. When the role-play is finished, give the groups a couple of minutes to share with each other their character descriptions.

LEADER You are the leader of the group. Your group has lots of needs, and you should try very hard to include everyone in the discussion and keep the discussion on track.

CHILD 1 You are an intelligent child who knows all the answers and keeps putting their hand up to answer, or to ask a question. You don't call out or interrupt, though.

CHILD 2 You are a very shy, younger child, who is very slow in interacting with the group.

CHILD 3 You are a 'fidgeter' who can't keep still, but you follow what is being discussed.

CHILD 4 You naturally interrupt all the time, but should respond to firm handling by your team leader. You should ask to go to the toilet at least once during the short group time.

CHILD 5 You listen well and follow all that your leader asks you to do, making a valuable contribution to the group.

CHILD 6 You are deeply committed to Jesus, and yet find it very difficult to articulate how you feel. You try very hard to contribute to the group.

FEEDBACK FROM THE ROLE PLAY
This activity is a good way of raising some of the issues involved in leading a small group. Have a flip chart or OHP acetate ready to note down any interesting points that come up.

Talk first to the group leaders, encouraging them that it will never be as difficult as this at **PYRAMID ROCK**! Ask them to outline the characters in their group. Who was difficult to deal with? Who contributed? Who didn't contribute? Do they know why?

Discuss some of the issues raised by the characters, for example how are you going to deal with children going to the toilet? By the time the feedback has finished, you should have a set of guidelines for leading a group. Below are a few dos and don'ts which may be worth adding to discussion at the end.

DOS AND DON'TS OF LEADING A SMALL GROUP
▲ Do learn their names quickly, and use them.
▲ Do take notice of how each child behaves, reacts and interacts, so you can get to know each one.
▲ Do take the initiative. Let them know clearly what you expect from the group, and how each member is valued and encouraged to participate.
▲ Do be specific in your prompting and questions – this can help everyone contribute.
▲ Do be aware that each child will come with their own needs.
▲ Do be polite and patient, even if one or two children really annoy you!
▲ Do add lots of enthusiasm to your group. The children will pick up on your attitude – you are a role model.
▲ Do think creatively, for example how you sit, lie, kneel as a group to discuss things.
▲ Do model what you expect the children to do, eg your response to what happens on the stage.
▲ Do be careful to follow closely any instructions or notes you are given.
▲ Do ask for help if you need it – you are not alone!
▲ Do be careful with language – no jargon, complicated or inappropriate language.
▲ Do pray for them and yourself as you lead the group.
▲ Don't have any favourites.
▲ Don't be physical with them, as physical involvement can be misinterpreted.

SECTION 3
Keeping control of your group

Give a few pointers on how to keep good control and behaviour within groups. You could split the team into small groups to come up with their top tips, or simply talk through some of the issues.

There are three general approaches to discipline:
▲ Aggressive discipline – lots of shouting and aggressive words and threats;
▲ Non-assertive discipline – pleading with the children to behave (the children feel in control with this sort of discipline);
▲ Assertive discipline – is where leaders calmly, lovingly, fairly and firmly insist that the club rules are followed. This is the best form of discipline and it would be good to discuss with the team how you are going to approach the various characters that will come to the holiday club. You will need to establish a set of ground rules for the club and for the building. You will need to make sure that each Pyramid Leader is aware of them, and able to support each other in the implementation of each rule. Make sure that these are recorded to ensure a safe, fun and successful week.

The key to establishing good discipline and control is relationship building and clear expectations. This can be done by:
▲ clearly stating and explaining expectations;
▲ rewarding good behaviour;
▲ praising them;
▲ telling them when they haven't reached your expectations, and why;
▲ explaining why clear boundaries are needed, and what would happen if everyone didn't follow the club rules;
▲ recognising the positive actions of a child who usually misbehaves and encouraging them to behave better.

We need to understand that behaviour can sometimes be affected by:
▲ physical factors, eg the room, or the temperature
▲ lack of preparation
▲ poor resources
▲ weather
▲ poor presentation of the programme
▲ disruptive influences
▲ what is going on at home
▲ tiredness
▲ personality clashes
▲ previous events in the club
▲ special needs, such as medical, behavioural, educational needs
▲ lack of leadership or the leader's own lack of confidence
▲ inconsistency of rules between leaders
▲ the children's unfamiliarity with clubs such as **PYRAMID ROCK**

SESSION 2

The children – final preparations

INTRODUCTION

SECTION 1 Sharing your faith with children
SECTION 2 Working with children with special needs
SECTION 3 Working with children from other faith backgrounds
SECTION 4 Praying with children
SECTION 5 Practical preparations
SECTION 6 Praying for **PYRAMID ROCK** and all who come or are involved

EQUIPMENT Flip chart and pens (or some other way of recording feedback and presenting material), OHP/data projector to show song lyrics and examples of the visuals to be used during the week

INTRODUCTION

Outline the aims and content of your time together.

RECAP

Recap on the training undertaken during the previous session. If you did not have time to look at the 'Keeping control of your group' section, you may wish to run through some of the key points at the beginning of this second session.

SECTION 1

Sharing your faith with children

An extended version of this section is on the DVD. The reason for this is that this feature of working with children is so important and one of the most demanding requirements of a children's worker. Sharing our faith with children is one of the greatest privileges we have as Christians. In 1 Peter 3:15, Peter encourages God's people to be ready to give an answer to anyone who asks about their faith.

The story of Joseph is found in the Old Testament and has some wonderful lessons for the children to learn. However, it will be through our conversations and testimonies with the children that they will understand what it means to be a Christian today.

Spend time thinking through some of the issues listed below and make full use of the DVD material. Whether or not you are using the DVD, give the team time to think about what they might say to the children and help them practise on each other!

TELLING STORIES

Children love real life stories – find some good stories to share, either contemporary ones or in films or literature, which illustrate God's character and impact on the world, such as the importance of forgiveness in making relationships.

Think about when you were the children's age. What relevant experiences do you have which are not introduced with the words, 'When I was a little boy and life was not as bad as it is now …' Alternatively, what experiences do you have now which illustrate, for example Joseph's trust in God when everything went wrong.

If you are leading a planned testimony from the front, always be careful to relate your testimony to the themes being discussed during the teaching programme and to the experiences of the children.

LANGUAGE

- Avoiding using jargon or complicated language with inappropriate vocabulary.
- Be careful not to use language that could be interpreted too literally, eg how do you explain Jesus living with and in us in a way that is not scary for a 6-year-old? An unseen person invited into our heart can sound terrifying!
- Remember actions speak louder than words – children look at how you act and react to them and to the other members of the team.
- Always tell the truth, and avoid exaggerating too much!

APPROACH

- Make your testimonies short and simple, not long and complicated!
- Have one main aim or focus.
- Do not be patronising.
- Be encouraging and expect God to use what you say!
- Avoid too much hell and damnation as this is not needed and will frighten the children!
- Use as many visuals as possible, and if possible be interactive!

FINALLY

If you are presenting to an audience, rather than a casual conversation, always practise your 'speech'.

Think about how what you have planned will be understood by the children. You are talking to those who already know Jesus and those who hardly know him at all!

SECTION 2
Working with children with special needs

WORKING WITH CHILDREN WITH SPECIAL NEEDS

Being prepared to include children with special needs can be a tremendous blessing to the children and their parents, as well as the group.

▲ Enjoy these children for their individuality, value and what they have to offer. Some children with special needs may have distinct areas of interest or talents that can be developed at appropriate times.
▲ Always find out as much information as possible about the child before the start – their likes/dislikes, strengths/weaknesses, particular needs and how best they can be included to make them feel safe and part of the group.
▲ Medical needs should be noted on the signed registration form. Pay special attention to the use of medication. Keep a record of medication given, noting time and quantity, initialled by two team members.
▲ Designate leaders to work one-to-one with children with challenging behaviour. Where appropriate, set up a buddy system so that extra team members are available to children needing extra help. As far as possible, keep children with disabilities with their own peer group. Give all children opportunities to join in the activities.
▲ Expect good behaviour from all children, but be tolerant of unusual behaviour, eg some children may need to fiddle with something.

▲ Ensure all the children know what is planned for the day. Give children a five-minute warning when an activity is about to finish. Some children may need to finish one activity before they can concentrate on another.
▲ Prepare each session with a range of abilities in mind. Think carefully about working with abstract ideas. These may be misunderstood and taken literally!
▲ Have a range of craft ideas. Check that you do not give a child with learning difficulties a task that is appropriate for their reading age but inappropriate for their actual age.
▲ If you have a child with hearing difficulties, make sure they sit near the front and that leaders have their face clearly on view (not lit from behind). If a loop system is available, check that it is working for this child. Discussing in small groups can be hard for deaf children. Try to reduce background noise.
▲ Do a risk assessment so that you are aware of any difficulties that may arise and take all possible action to avoid these.

Talk these through with the team as appropriate, and discuss any known children with special needs for whom you are going to provide care.

SECTION 3
Working with children from other faith backgrounds

WORKING WITH CHILDREN FROM OTHER FAITHS

PRINCIPLES TO WORK FROM

▲ We will not criticise, ridicule or belittle other religions.
▲ We will not tell the children what their faith says or define it by what some of its adherents do.
▲ We will not ask children to say, sing or pray things that they do not believe or that compromise their own faith.
▲ We will respect the faith of the children.
▲ We will value and acknowledge the children's culture.
▲ We will use music, artwork and methods that are culturally appropriate.
▲ We will be open and honest in our presentation of the Christian faith.
▲ We will be open and honest about the content of our work with parents and other significant adults.
▲ We will seek to build long-term friendships that are genuine and not dependent upon conversion.
▲ Where children show a genuine interest in the Christian faith, we will encourage them, but be open and honest about the possible consequences. We will never encourage them to make decisions that could put them in danger.

There are some practical considerations.
▲ Many Asian communities (of all faiths, including Christian) are uncomfortable with bodily contact, especially between boys and girls. Does this mean you need to rethink your games? Moreover, many Asian girls may prefer to be in single-sexed groups. Make allowances for this.
▲ Be culturally sensitive about the food you offer – no pork products (including gelatine) for Muslims, while some Hindus don't eat eggs. Include a choice of snacks from various cultures.
▲ Acknowledge that children from other faith backgrounds have some understanding about the nature and person of God. Don't assume they know nothing or that what they know is wrong.
▲ Be open about what goes on in **PYRAMID ROCK**. Never suggest children keep things a secret.
▲ Remember that asking children to change faith may be dangerous or inappropriate – it could mean exclusion from the family or even death.

SECTION 4
Praying with children

Talk through the notes below with the team, and make specific arrangements for your **PYRAMID ROCK** week to allow children the space to pray.

When praying with children in a larger group or all together, take care to use simple, clear, modern English. Keep your prayers brief, relevant and free from jargon. At the end of the session, thank God for the time you have had together, the friendships made and the things learnt. As the week progresses, you may want to pray all together about things that worry the children or that are in the news. Talking with God should be very natural and the children need to realise this. Explain that we say 'Amen' as a means of saying we agree. We don't have to close our eyes and put our hands together!

Some children may ask for prayer individually, or desire to respond to God by praying by themselves. Pray with a child in the main hall where you can be seen, ideally in a designated quiet area. If their request comes at an inconvenient time, make sure you find time to be with the child later, or pass them on to a team member who is free.

A child may want to make a commitment to Jesus, maybe for the first or tenth time! Ask the child if they have any questions, and talk about the important step they are about to make. Explain clearly and simply what it means to follow Jesus. Pray a simple prayer with them, pausing to allow them to repeat each phrase out loud. An example of such a prayer is below.

> Jesus, I want to be your friend.
> Thank you that you love me.
> Thank you for living in the world and dying on a cross for me.
> I'm sorry for all the wrong things I have done.
> Please forgive me and let me be your friend.
> Please let the Holy Spirit help me be more like you.
> Amen

Assure the child that God hears us when we pray to him, and that he promises to forgive us and help us be his friends if we really want to. You may wish to photocopy the prayer on to a piece of card, with space for the child's name and the date. This prayer is also available as a commitment card to be downloaded from the eye level website: www.scriptureunion.org.uk/eyelevel Encourage them to show it to their parent or carer when they get home, if that is appropriate. Make sure they know about all the other activities that the church runs for children in their age group. Details of commitment booklets for specific ages are on the inside front cover.

Friends with Jesus
5 to 7s

Jesus=friendship forever
10 to 12s

Me + Jesus
8 to 9s

SECTION 5
Practical preparations for the week

Talk though a typical day with the team, helping them understand each part of the programme and what is expected of them throughout the session.

If possible, give the actors who play Captain Ketchup and the characters from the story an opportunity to introduce themselves. This will be fun, and will help the team get a feel for both the teaching and the sillier elements of the programme. If you have the time and space, play one or two of the games and learn the song.

Show them an episode of the **PYRAMID ROCK DVD** if you are using it.

Make sure that each team member is confident in their role and aware of everything they need to bring with them and of all the practicalities involved.

SECTION 6
Prayer

It is a good idea to produce a small prayer card for the members of your church to inform their prayers. Hand these out and ask the team to pray in small groups for the whole club, the leaders, children and all the preparations. Pray big, bold prayers of faith for what Jesus is going to do at **PYRAMID ROCK**!

PART 5
RESOURCE BANK

MEMORY VERSE

Traditionally, when Jewish children learnt the scriptures, they sang them! It remains one of the best ways for children to learn and memorise the scriptures. **PYRAMID ROCK DVD** contains one memory verse song for the whole week. This is Acts 7:9,10, which summarises the life of Joseph and his role in God's big plan.

> Joseph's brothers were jealous of him and sold him as a slave to be taken to Egypt. But God was with him and rescued him from all his troubles.
> Acts 7:9,10

MEMORY VERSE SONG

In Acts chapter 7 verses 9 and 10,
The Bible reminds us about Joseph again!
It says,
'His brothers were jealous of Joseph
And sold him as a slave,
To be taken to Egypt.
But God was with (young) Joseph
And rescued him,
Rescued him from all his troubles!'

Dave Godfrey © Scripture Union 2005
The music for the memory verse song is on the website: www.scriptureunion.org.uk/pyramidrock

SUGGESTED ACTIONS

In Acts chapter 7 verses 9 and 10,
Show 7, then 9, then 10 fingers.
The Bible reminds us about Joseph again!
Open hands as if opening a book then point to place on far side of room that can represent 'Egypt'.
It says, 'His brothers were jealous of Joseph
Lean back with hands folded, nodding. Then lean forward and draw a letter 'J' in the air on the word 'Joseph'.
And sold him as a slave,
One hand (on 'sold'), then the other hand (on 'slave') down in front of body as if being handcuffed.
To be taken to Egypt.
Keep hands together as you take two small steps forward on the 'taken' and 'Egypt'.
But God was with (young) Joseph
Point up to the sky and then draw a 'J' in the air.
And rescued him,
Hands back as in handcuffs on 'rescued' and 'him'.
Rescued him from all his troubles!'
Raise arms above head and 'break out' from the handcuffs. Wave arms about in celebration.

Alternatively, you could introduce the memory verse using other ideas. Here are a few to start you off:
▲ Write each word on a balloon. Pop each one as the children say the verse, until they can remember it.
▲ Put all the words on different pieces of card. Have a washing line going across the room, with the cards pegged to it (maybe cut out in the shape of clothing). Gradually take the pieces of card down as the children learn the verse.
▲ Photocopy the memory verse onto card, cut it up and give it to the groups as a jigsaw puzzle. The children can learn the verse in groups and tell the rest of the club what they have learnt.
▲ Put the memory verse on acetate in non-permanent pen. Read it through a few times and then rub out some of the words. Repeat until the whole memory verse has been rubbed off.

On each day's Pyramid Piece (see inside front cover), the younger children will find a copy of the memory verse. This will mean they can practise it at home. The Pyramid Pieces contain the full memory verse from the CEV Bible. The memory verse song is a slight paraphrase of these verses. Decide which version you are going to use and stick with that.

PYRAMID ROCK

We're gonna swim up the Nile,
We're gonna open the scroll,
We're gonna have some fun as we get to know about Joseph,
The Hebrew boy called Joseph.
We're gonna ride on a camel,
Gonna dance in the sand.
We're gonna see what God was doing in the land of Egypt,
The mighty, mighty land of Egypt,
'Cause Joseph and his God made the pyramids rock!
So sing and dance at the pyramid rock,
Jump and jive at the pyramid rock,
Celebrate at the pyramid rock,
'Cause Joseph and his God made the pyramids rock!

Dave Godfrey © Scripture Union 2005

SUGGESTED ACTIONS TO 'PYRAMID ROCK'

For the intro, hand jive: cross flat hands (palms facing floor) with right above left twice. Repeat with left above right. Touch fingers of left hand to right elbow, hold right forearm vertically and circle right index finger. Repeat with opposite hands so you are circling left index finger. Repeat everything 3 more times.

We're gonna swim up the Nile,
'Front crawl' arms.

We're gonna open the scroll,
Hands as if holding a scroll. Move left hand down whilst moving right hand up to 'open' scroll.

We're gonna have some fun as we get to know about Joseph,
Hand jive, starting on 'have': cross flat hands (palms facing floor) with right above left twice. Repeat with left above right. Touch fingers of left hand to right elbow, hold right forearm vertically and circle right index finger. Repeat with opposite hands so you are circling left index finger. Point to left twice with left thumb (like thumbing for a lift).

The Hebrew boy called Josep.
Repeat as above for 'get to know about Joseph.'

We're gonna ride on a camel,
Knees bent out to sides, fists circling vertically in front (like riding a horse).

Gonna dance in the sand,
Starting on 'dance': hop on left foot, then kick right leg. Hop on right foot, then kick left foot.

We're gonna see what God was doing in the land of Egypt,
Hand jive, starting on 'see': cross flat hands (palms facing floor) with right above left twice, repeat with left above right. Touch fingers of left hand to right elbow, hold right forearm vertically and circle right index finger. Repeat with opposite hands so you are circling left index finger (as for intro). Point to right twice with right thumb (like thumbing for a lift).

The mighty, mighty land of Egypt,
Repeat as above for 'doing in the land of Egypt'.

'Cause Joseph and his God made the pyramids rock!
'Thumb' left once on 'Joseph', point up with right index finger on 'God'. Rotate forearms with clenched fists round each other at chest height, then point left arm diagonally down and point right arm diagonally up (an Elvis-style pose!).

So sing and dance at the pyramid rock,
Free dance, then as above for 'pyramid rock'.

Jump and jive at the pyramid rock,
Cross flat hands (palms facing floor) with right above left once. Repeat with left above right. Match the hand movements by jumping with the feet, crossing them and opening them twice. Then repeat as before for 'pyramid rock'.

Celebrate at the pyramid rock,
Do 'the twist' down and up. Then as before for 'pyramid rock'.

'Cause Joseph and his God made the pyramids rock!
As before.

Instrumental: *Egyptian dance – 8 left, 8 right, 4 left, 4 right.*

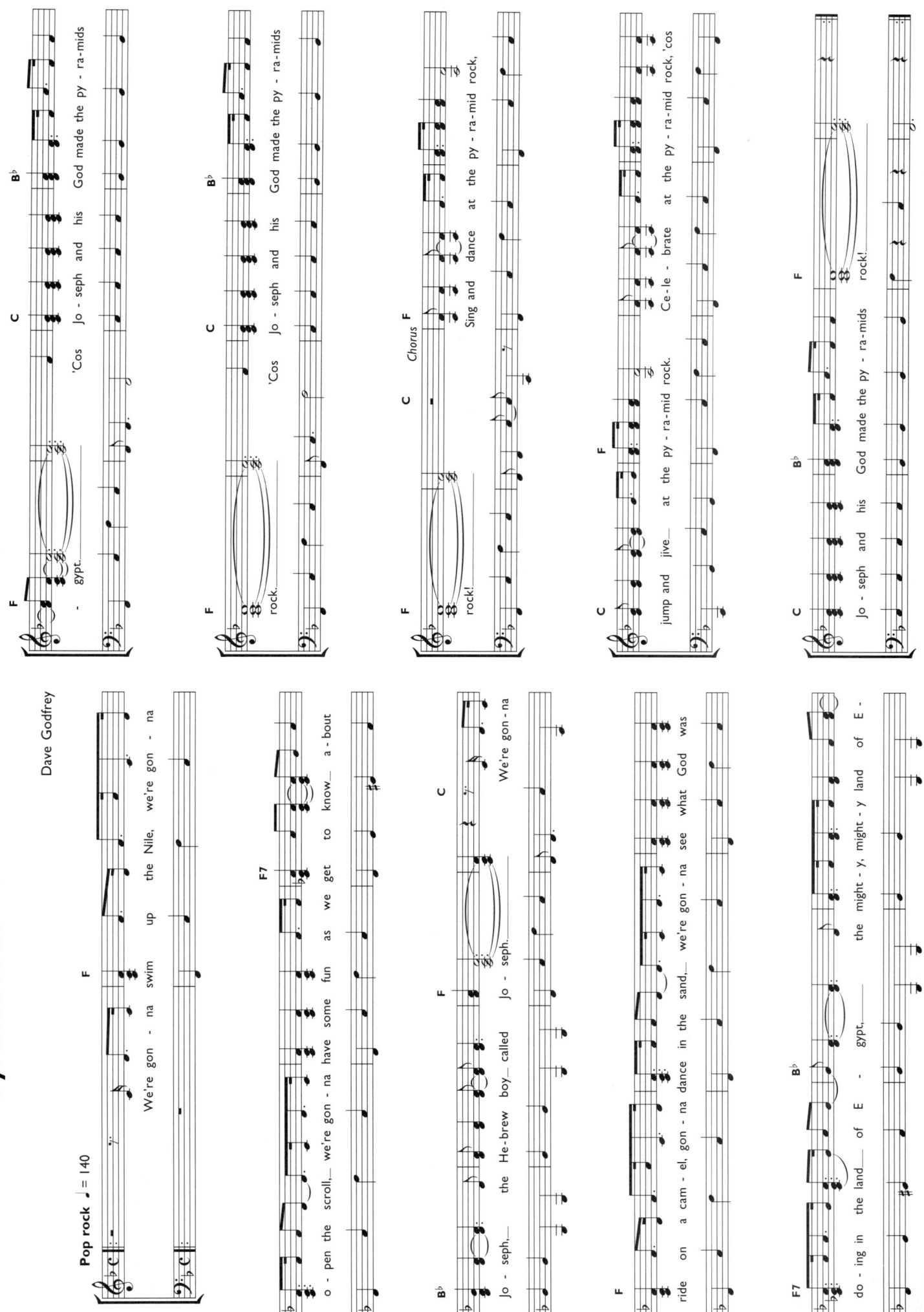

THE ADVENTURES OF DR POTTY

INTRODUCTION

This is the story of a mad archaeologist (Dr Potty) and his niece (Denise) who go in search of an ancient artefact that dates back to the time of Joseph. It is very slapstick and silly in style, but it deliberately plays on the key words and themes for each day. I hope you enjoy the story and the fun of these seven sketches!

MAIN CHARACTERS
DR POTTY A somewhat mad inventor/archaeologist, who wears a white lab coat and a long multicoloured scarf.

DENISE The niece of Dr Potty. She is fun-loving and a lot more sensible than Dr. Potty! She wears a dress for sketches A and 1, then normal, everyday clothing for all the other sketches.

OTHER CHARACTERS
PRINCESS POTTY (We never actually meet this character!) She is the younger sister of Dr Potty and Auntie to Denise. She has just married into the Egyptian royal family.

POSTMAN PETE (Episodes 1 and 3) The local postman who knows Denise and Dr Potty very well. He needs to wear a suitable postman costume.

MUMMY (Episodes 2 and 5) A mime character who comes on dressed up in toilet rolls to look like a mummy.

MARI-ANNE (Episode 2) A French chef who is on holiday in Egypt.

MAIN PROPS

1 'Relic with the Missing Onion-Shaped Piece' and the missing piece from the 'Relic with the Missing Onion-Shaped Piece'. This can be made out of plastic sheeting, wood or something else with some strength in it. The main relic should be shaped like an Egyptian urn with an onion-shaped piece missing from the middle.

Written on the relic is the message: 'You tried to h [onion piece gap] but God made it turn out [onion piece gap]'.

Written on the missing onion piece is: 'arm me … for the best'.

The complete message is: 'You tried to harm me but God made it turn out for the best' Genesis 50:20.

2 Five decoy missing pieces, which are identical in shape to the real missing piece. These pieces do not carry any message and are needed on Day 2 and Day 5.

3 The 'Relic Detector'. This is a simple detection device, made from the following equipment:
▲ a plastic bowl/container with a hole in (for connection to a vacuum cleaner hose) and a small dial mounted on it;
▲ an old vacuum cleaner hose (or something similar) to fit onto the bowl;
▲ an old vacuum cleaner brush which fits on the end of the vacuum cleaner hose;
▲ a small rucksack which Dr Potty wears that has a thin tube sticking out of it also connected to the bowl;
▲ anything else you might wish to add to 'soup up' the 'Relic Detector'!

EPISODE A
DR POTTY AND THE WEDDING
Use in Family Service A

THEME
Promise

SUMMARY
We are introduced to the characters of Dr Potty and his niece, Denise. Both of them are getting ready for the wedding of Princess Potty, Dr Potty's sister and Denise's auntie. Dr Potty has written a promise to his sister, wrapped it around an onion and placed it in a box. Denise is all dressed up and ready for the wedding, and has to find some clothes from her dressing up box for Dr Potty. Dr Potty and Denise go off to the wedding wondering how Princess Potty will respond to the promise from Dr Potty.

COSTUMES
Denise Smart wedding clothes
Dr Potty Lab coat, long multicoloured scarf and dressing-up clothes (wig, jacket, glasses, hat etc)

PROPS
Big cardboard box, wrapped in wedding paper
Big dressing-up box with the dressing-up clothes in

SOUND EFFECTS
Church bells

SKETCH
Dr Potty enters in lab coat and multicoloured scarf and carrying a massive wedding present. He starts singing.

Dr Potty 'We're getting married in the morning, ding-dong the bells are going to chime!' Oh I can't wait – this is just so exciting! (Dr Potty puts down box on one side of stage, then spots everyone watching.) Hi, everyone – my name's…
Denise (Entering at speed, dressed for the wedding and cutting Dr Potty off in mid sentence.) Morning, Dr Potty!
Dr Potty That's right, my name is 'Morning, Dr Potty'! (Pauses and thinks.) No it's not!
Denise You said it!
Dr Potty I'm Dr Potty! I'm an archaeologist – I dig things up!
Denise Hi everyone. My name's Denise, and I'm his niece!
Dr Potty 'We're getting married in the morning, ding-dong the bells are going to chime!'
Denise Dr Potty, we're not getting married, it's your sister and my auntie who's getting married.
Dr Potty How can my sister and your auntie be getting married? They are both women!
Denise Your sister is my auntie – she's the same person, and she's getting married to the Egyptian Prince and becoming part of the royal family. (Lifts her head and right arm in dramatic pose.) She's going to be known as…
Dr Potty (In a deep manly voice.) 'Princess Potty'!
Denise And we'd better get a move on so we don't miss the wedding. What's in the box, Dr Potty? (Goes over to the box.) It's really smelly!
Dr Potty It's a very special wedding present for my little sister!
Denise Has it got your smelly socks in or something?
Dr Potty Nope, something much nicer than that!
Denise What is it then?
Dr Potty A promise!
Denise It's a very smelly promise!
Dr Potty It's a promise written on a piece of paper and I've wrapped it around an onion!
Denise A promise written on a piece of paper and wrapped around an onion?!
Dr Potty Yep, cos here in Egypt, going back over many years, when you make a promise to someone you have to be holding an onion!
Denise Really?
Dr Potty Yep, and seeing as I won't be with her when she opens this big present, I've tied my promise around one of my smelly onions.
Denise Oh! What does the promise say?
Dr Potty It says, 'Dear Princess Potty, for your wedding present, I promise to do anything you ask me to do! Lots of love, Dr Potty!'
Denise That's a great idea, Dr Potty. She might ask you to shave her head every day! (She demonstrates.)
Dr Potty If she does, I'll fulfil my promise!
Denise She might ask you to eat a rotten onion!
Dr Potty Uggh!
Denise Only teasing! Anyway, we'd better get to the wedding.
Dr Potty You look fantastic, Denise.
Denise You look terrible – you can't go to the wedding in your lab coat. It's a good job my dressing-up box is just over here.

Denise goes straight to her dressing-up box, on the side of the stage, and starts handing Dr Potty a few silly things like a wig, silly glasses, jacket etc – all of which make him look very silly! When complete…

Dr Potty How do I look?
Denise You look ridiculous! Hold on, what's that sound I can hear? (Sound effect: Church bells.)
Denise Come on, time's up!
Dr Potty OK Denise, I'll grab the present! I wonder what Princess Potty will ask me to do. It's going to be an

exciting time when we find out!

Denise (To audience, in heroic type voice.) My name is Denise and his name is Dr Potty.

Dr Potty (To audience, in the same voice.) You've been watching the Adventures of Dr Potty. Next episode tomorrow*, bye! (* State day of next episode.)

Denise and Dr Potty leave.

Dr Potty (Starts singing.) 'We're getting married in the morning'

Denise (Shouts from off-stage.) Oh no, we're not!

DAY 1
DR POTTY AND THE ULTIMATE CHALLENGE

THEME
Jealousy

SUMMARY
Dr Potty and Denise come in discussing the wedding of Princess Potty. Denise introduces them both to the children, but Dr Potty has become very jealous of Princess Potty. Postman Pete arrives with two letters and a parcel for Dr Potty. The parcel is an ancient relic, and the second letter is from Princess Potty asking Dr Potty to begin a new search to solve the 'Secret of the Secret Message' by finding the missing piece of the 'Relic with the Missing Onion Shaped Piece'. The missing piece is in the shape of an onion! Denise and Dr Potty accept the challenge and leave so that they can get ready to start the search the following morning.

COSTUMES
Denise Smart wedding clothes
Dr Potty Lab coat, long multicoloured scarf and dressing up clothes (wig, jacket, glasses, hat etc)
Postman Pete A postman's uniform

PROPS
2 letters
The Relic, wrapped up in brown parcel paper

SOUND EFFECTS
None

SKETCH
Dr Potty and Denise stumble in, still dressed in their wedding stuff.

Denise What a fantastic wedding!

Dr Potty (Starts to take off the extra dressing up bits – hat, wig, glasses, and so on. You will not need to use these if you did not use Episode A.) Princess Potty, your aunt, looked beautiful.

Denise Did you give her that really big present?

Dr Potty You mean the box with the onion inside?

Denise Yep, the box with the onion that had the piece of paper tied around it!

Dr Potty You mean the piece of paper which said, 'Dear Princess Potty, for your wedding present, I promise to do anything you ask me to do! Lots of love, Doctor Potty!'

Denise Yes!

Dr Potty (Pause.) Yep!

Denise Did you see her open it?

Dr Potty (Pause.) No!

Denise Oh well! She did look really pretty though.

Dr Potty (Towards the end of the sentence Dr Potty starts to speak in a slightly negative tone.) Isn't it is amazing; Princess Potty – your auntie, and my sister, now being part of the royal family!

Denise Yep. Look Dr Potty, there's lots of people here. Hi everyone, my name's Denise and I'm his niece! Say, 'Hi!' Dr Potty.

Dr Potty (Has a very quick change in attitude and answers in a very lack-lustre way.) Hi.

Denise What's wrong, Dr Potty?

Dr Potty Oh, nothing.

Denise Come on, Dr Potty, you're not called Dr Potty for nothing. You're a mad archaeologist who is always jolly and making people laugh. What's wrong?

Dr Potty Not much! (He goes and sits down on the floor, or on a table at the side of the stage!)

Denise After such a happy time at the wedding, you can't be in a bad mood today. (Denise walks over in a friendly sort of a way.) Dr Potty I'm your friend as well as your niece. There's just you, me, and a few friendly people over there. Go on, tell me what's wrong.

Dr Potty (Gets up and starts pacing. The next bit needs to be said in a jealous tone.) Well, it's just that Princess Potty, my little sister, is now married to the Prince. She is now part of the royal family. She'll have loads of money, and things, and servants and… and she'll be famous for ever. And I'm just a mad archaeologist who finds old things by digging them up. She is really famous, and no-one knows who I am!

Denise Well, if you were to ask me what I think…

Pyramid Leaders 'What do you think, Denise?' (Ready the team beforehand to shout this.)

Dr Potty Oh, that was good, wasn't it, but I didn't hear many children shouting – shall we try that line again with the children joining in as well this time?

Denise Well, if you were to ask me what I think…

Children What do you think Denise?

Denise Glad you asked me. I think, Dr Potty, you're jealous!

Dr Potty No, I'm not!

Denise I think you are! You're jealous of your sister! You should be really pleased for her!

Dr Potty Huh!

Denise You need to think about your attitude. If you stay jealous, you might find yourself saying something, or doing something that you regret!

Dr Potty Maybe!

Denise Anyway, we think you're great and there's no need to be jealous. Hold on, I think I can smell your onion again, Dr Potty!

Postman Pete (Walks in holding a big triangular shaped parcel and two letters for Dr Potty.) 'Postman Pete, Postman Pete, Postman Pete and his stinky feet. Early in the morning, just as day is dawning, you can smell him coming down your street!' Morning Dr Potty, morning Denise, morning everyone!

Denise Morning Pete, is that a new song then?

Postman Pete Do you like it? It goes, 'Postman Pete, Postman Pete, Postman Pete and his stinky feet. (Holds nose.) Early in the morning, just as day is dawning, you can smell him coming down your street!' Tell you what, I'll go away again for a moment, you say that onion line again, and I'll come back in. Then we can all join in the song! (To audience.) Will you help children?

Denise I think I can smell your onion again Dr Potty!

Postman Pete (Walks in, still holding a big triangular shaped parcel and two letters for Dr Potty.) 'Postman Pete, Postman Pete, Postman Pete and his stinky feet. Early in the morning, just as day is dawning, you can smell him coming down your street!' That's great. I've got some post for you Dr Potty! (Hands over parcel and two letters to Dr Potty who accepts them.)

Dr Potty Thanks Pete. (Pete leaves.)

Denise Go on, open them!

Dr Potty OK, erm, let's go for this letter first. (Opens first letter.) Oh it's from Mrs Potty, my wife. It says, 'Dear Dr Potty, I just wanted to say that I really love you and thought you looked really handsome at the wedding yesterday! Lots of love Mrs P.'

Denise Ahh, a love letter from your wife!

Dr Potty That's cheered me up a bit! Let's go for the parcel next! It looks like a pyramid!'

Denise If it's a pyramid, I wonder who's buried inside it.

Dr Potty It has to be someone very thin.

Denise Maybe it's someone who used to live in a flat!

Dr Potty (Finally gets inside parcel.) Wow, if I'm not mistaken, this is a very precious ancient relic. It's known as 'The Relic with the Missing Onion Shaped Piece'. It's very precious; I wonder who has sent it to me?

Denise Maybe the other letter will tell you.

Dr Potty OK, let's open that too. Oh, it's from Princess Potty. It says, 'Dear Dr Potty, thank you very much for your lovely wedding present. As soon as I read your promise, I knew immediately what to ask you to do. Please can you use all your amazing archaeological skills to make one more desperate attempt to solve the 'Secret of the Secret Message', which is written on the 'Relic with the Missing Onion Shaped Piece'. I have sent you the ancient relic in a parcel. I couldn't think of anyone better to solve this ancient mystery. Find it and you will be handsomely rewarded. Lots of love, Princess Potty.'

Denise Wow! Hasn't this mystery baffled historians down the centuries?

Dr Potty If we found the onion shaped piece, we would be able to read the secret message written by Pharaoh all those years ago.

Denise What does the relic say?

Dr Potty It says, 'You tried to, but God made it turn out' If we find the missing piece, it will probably tell us why God turned it out!

Denise That's amazing!

Dr Potty This relic is from about 1660 BC, so it's really, really old. Our mission is simple! We need to solve the 'Secret of the Secret Message' by finding the missing piece from the the 'Relic with the Missing Onion Shaped Piece'.

Denise This is your opportunity to become fam—

Dr Potty (Interrupting Denise.) Sshh! This is my opportunity to become famous, Denise!

Denise We should go and get ready for the sear—

Dr Potty (Interrupting again.) Wait! We should go and get ready for the search, Denise.

Denise (To audience, in heroic type voice.) My name is Denise and his name is Dr Potty.

Dr Potty (To audience, in same voice.) You've been watching the Adventures of Dr Potty. The search begins tomorrow*, bye! (* State day of next episode.)

Denise and Dr Potty leave.

Dr Potty (Starts singing.) 'We're getting married in the morning'

Denise (Shouts from off-stage.) Oh no, we're not; we're going searching in the morning!

DAY 2
DR POTTY AND THE ONION BISCUITS

THEME
Helper

SUMMARY
Dr Potty starts to plan how to find the piece of relic but he soon feels all alone. Denise comes in to help but they are having difficulty knowing where to start. Dr Potty consults his Mummy but she isn't much help. He then suggests that they have something to eat. A famous French chef called Mari-Anne happens to pop in and together they have a go at making some of 'Old Uncle Arthur's onion biscuits'. This leads to a bit of chaos but eventually they produce some excellent biscuits. Amazingly these biscuits are the exact shape and texture of the missing piece from the 'Relic with the Missing Onion Shaped Piece'. One biscuit fits perfectly, but sadly does not reveal the 'Secret of the Secret Message' written by the ancient Pharaoh – because it is a biscuit! The search continues…

COSTUMES
Denise Normal, everyday clothes
Dr Potty Lab coat and long multicoloured scarf
Mummy Someone completely dressed up in toilet rolls
Mari-Anne A French chef who is on holiday in Egypt

PROPS
Child's hanging mobile
Long piece of rope, which is held behind a screen by someone who pretends to be a bull!
Two identical bowls
Relic biscuits
Eggs, Flour, Milk, Salt
Oven (either a box on stage or an imaginary oven off-stage)
Recipe card or book
Boxer shorts
Protective floor covering (such as plastic sheeting)

SOUND EFFECTS
Bull

SKETCH
Dr Potty (Walks in singing.) 'I'm going searching in the morning!' Morning everyone!
Children Morning Dr Potty! (This may need practising!)
Dr Potty This morning we start the search for the onion shaped piece that is missing from the 'Relic with the Missing Onion Shaped Piece'. When we find it we will be able to solve the 'Secret of the Secret Message' which is written on it! (Starts talking to himself.) Right. Where shall we start? I know, I'll look under my bed! No that's ridiculous – that's where my smelly socks go, not relics. Maybe… Maybe… Oh where is Denise when I need her? I feel all alone – I need a helper on this mission. I know, I'll ring her on my mobile. (Brings out a child's hanging mobile from his pocket and starts talking to it!) Denise! Denise!
Denise (Appearing on stage. Dr Potty has his back to her and continues to talk to the mobile.) Yes Dr Potty?
Dr Potty Denise I feel so alone, please can you help me?
Denise Of course I will.
Dr Potty I'm currently down where we left the relic. When will you be able to get here?
Denise Count to 20 and I'll be there!
Dr Potty 1, 2, 3, 4, 5, 6, 7, 8, 9, 10, 11, 12, 13, 14, 15, 16, 17, 18, 19, 20! (During countdown Denise goes walking around the stage making stamping noises as though she is getting closer. On 20 Dr Potty turns around.) Oh there you are!
Denise I've been here all the time!
Dr Potty (Pausing for dramatic effect.) Are you sure?
Denise I was here all the time, wasn't I children?
Children Yes!
Dr Potty Oh no you weren't!
Children Oh yes she was! (This carries on for a while.)
Dr Potty Well, I wonder why I didn't see you! Anyway, we'd better get on with the search.
Denise Where are we going to start, Dr Potty?
Dr Potty I don't know. I thought about looking under my bed, but then that's stupid. I think we should sit down and make a plan!
Dr Potty and Denise sit down and after 20 seconds of head scratching, Dr Potty stands up.
Dr Potty I think we should ask my mummy for some advice! (Shouts.) Mummy!
Mummy walks onto centre of stage and remains relatively static and silent when talked to by Dr Potty.
Dr Potty What do you think we should do Mummy? Where should we start? Oh this is useless, Mummy doesn't know either!
Denise Well, if you were to ask me what I think…
Children What do you think Denise!
Denise Glad you asked me, I think we need some food inside us. The energy from the food will help us to plan!
Mari-Anne (Appearing back stage, somewhat sheepishly.) Hello, did someone say food?
Denise Who are you?
Mari-Anne My name is Mari-Anne, I am a famous French chef and I am here in Egypt on holiday. I am

desperate to try one of these ancient Egyptian recipes. Would you help me?

Dr Potty That would be great! We could help you cook, and you can help us by letting us eat the food!

Denise What are we going to cook?

Mari-Anne I have found this ancient recipe for 'Old Uncle Arthur's onion biscuits'

Dr Potty 'Old Uncle Arthur's onion biscuits' – sounds great. What do we need?

Mari-Anne We need a table.

Denise Oh dear, we haven't got a table!

Dr Potty Mummy will help! Come over here Mummy. (Puts Mummy onto her hands and knees, with her back flat to act as a table.)

Mari-Anne We need a bowl. (She says 'bowl' so that it sounds like 'bull'.)

Denise I think I saw one outside. (Goes off to side of stage and pulls on a thick rope – sound effect of bull.)

Mari-Anne Non, non, stupids! I said a bowl!

Denise Oh, here's one. (Hands Mari-Anne the bowl.) What else do we need?

Mari-Anne Hen's eggs. Une, (Cracks one on Mummy's head.) Oops, deux. (Cracks one in the bowl.)

Denise Here's some milk!

Mari-Anne We need to add the flour in like so, and add a pinch— (Denise pinches Dr Potty.)

Dr Potty Ow, not that sort of pinch!

Mari-Anne —of salt! Now we cook it! (Takes bowl off the back of Mummy and puts it into the oven.)

Dr Potty How long does it take the biscuits to cook?

Mari-Anne (Checking recipe.) About ten seconds.

Denise They must be done by now, then!

Mari-Anne (Going off and brings back an identical bowl with the finished biscuits.) Voila!

Dr Potty Hey look – they really are onion shaped biscuits!

Denise Incredible!

Dr Potty Amazing!

Denise (Thinking hard.) Hey!

Dr Potty (Also thinking hard.) Hey!

Denise (Getting really excited.) Hey!

Dr Potty This small biscuit is almost the same shape and texture of the missing piece from the 'Relic with the Missing Onion Shaped Piece.'

Denise Let's try it!

Dr Potty (Carefully placing the biscuit into the relic.) It fits!

Denise It fits!

Dr Potty We've found the missing piece!

Denise, Dr Potty and Mari-Anne all hug each other! Whilst they are still hugging…

Denise Hold on!

Dr Potty I am holding on.

Denise No. (Everyone lets go.) If you were to ask me what I think…

Children What do you think Denise?

Denise Glad you asked me, I think that biscuit might fit the relic, but it's not the right piece.

Dr Potty Why not?

Denise Because, look at it. It does not tell us the 'Secret of the Secret Message'.

Dr Potty Rats!

Mari-Anne Where? Arrrrgh! I hate rats! (Runs off.)

Denise (Shouting after the departed Mari-Anne.) Thank you Mari-Anne for coming to help us! Listen – it's getting late. I'll have a look on the Internet and see if I can find some clues. We'll meet here in the morning, Dr Potty – same time and we'll start again! OK?

Dr Potty OK!

Denise (To audience, in heroic type voice.) My name is Denise, his name is Dr Potty and that's his mummy.

Dr Potty (To audience, in the same voice.) You've been watching the Adventures of Dr Potty. The search continues tomorrow*, bye! (* State day of next episode.)

Denise, Dr Potty and Mummy leave.

Dr Potty (Singing.) 'We're cooking Mummy in the morning'

Denise (Shouting from off-stage.) Your poor mummy!

DAY 3
DR POTTY AND THE ONION DETECTOR

THEME
Provision

SUMMARY
Denise comes in all excited; she has found an amazing website: www.egyptianrelic.net. The website shows how to make an amazing relic detection device. She has printed off the instructions and ordered the parts. When these are delivered by Postman Pete, Denise and Dr Potty create a special 'Relic Detector'! When the Relic Detector is turned on, it begins to lead them into new and interesting situations, and takes them a step closer to finding the missing piece of relic!

COSTUMES
Denise Normal, everyday clothes
Dr Potty Lab coat and long multicoloured scarf
Postman Pete Postman's uniform

PYRAMID ROCK

PROPS

Piece of paper with instructions on
The Relic Detector parts packaged as below (see introduction for more details)
Parcel 1 – Bowl or plastic container
Parcel 2 – Hose and gaffer tape
Parcel 3 – Brush end of tubing
Parcel 4 – Ruck-sack with small tube (or string) to connect to bowl

SOUND EFFECTS

Low level noise when the Relic Detector is working

SKETCH

Denise (Walking in, looking at instructions.) Just wait till Dr Potty sees this! Good morning, everyone!

Children Morning, Denise!

Denise (Talking to children.) I went on this amazing website yesterday and it gave me a great idea!

Dr Potty (Walking in.) Good morning, Potty fans!

Children Morning, Dr Potty!

Dr Potty Morning Denise, what have you got there?

Denise You're going to like this, Dr Potty – it's instructions to make a Relic Detector – I got it off www.egyptianrelic.net on the Internet!

Dr Potty (Shocked and suddenly very interested.) Wow! Hey, that's great. Let's see if we can build it then!

Denise We'll have to wait a few minutes.

Dr Potty Why?

Denise I ordered the bits, but they haven't arrived yet!

Dr Potty Can you smell onions?

Postman Pete (Walking in holding the first of the parcels.) 'Postman Pete, Postman Pete, Postman Pete and his stinky feet. Early in the morning, just as day is dawning, you can smell him coming down your street!' Morning Dr Potty, morning Denise, morning everyone!

Denise That must be it!

Postman Pete This is the first of about four parcels for you. I'll have to go back and get the other ones! See you in a minute.

Dr Potty Thanks, Pete. Let's open parcel one. It must contain the first important part of the Relic detector!

Denise (Looking inside.) Oh look – it's a plastic bowl! The instructions say 'The Saucer Section'

Dr Potty It's got a big hole in the side, a small hole in the top and a dial! Very intriguing. Oh, and it smells of onions!

Postman Pete (Walking in holding the second of the parcels.) 'Postman Pete, Postman Pete, Postman Pete and his stinky feet. Early in the morning, just as day is dawning, you can smell him coming down your street!' Here's parcel two – back in a minute!

Dr Potty I wonder what's in this one!

Denise The instructions say it should be 'The Wiggly Hose' section.

Dr Potty Ah yes, here it is.

Denise It fits into the Saucer Section like this. (Makes it fit, securing it with tape also found in parcel 2.) This tape smells funny!

Postman Pete (Walking in holding the third of the parcels.) 'Postman Pete, Postman Pete, Postman Pete and his stinky feet. Early in the morning, just as day is dawning, you can smell him coming down your street!' OK you two, here's parcel three!

Dr Potty What does it say this is?

Denise 'The Sensor Section'

Dr Potty (Taking it out of parcel 3.) Oh, it looks remarkably like the brush bit on my vacuum cleaner!

Denise I think it goes right here. (Places it on the end of the Wiggly Hose section.)

Dr Potty Perfect! Right, let's see if we can make it work? (Pauses waiting for it to work.) There doesn't seem to be anything happening

Denise Well if you were to ask me what I think…

Children What do you think, Denise?

Denise Glad you asked me. I think it won't work yet because it needs batteries. I can smell those onions again – they must be in parcel four!

Postman Pete (Walking in holding the fourth parcel.) 'Postman Pete, Postman Pete, Postman Pete and his stinky feet. Early in the morning, just as day is dawning, you can smell him coming down your street!' That's the last one. Bye!

Denise Thanks Pete.

Dr Potty Let's have a look at what's in here.

Denise It should be a battery pack and 'The Juice Distributor'.

Dr Potty Looks like it. I'll pop the pack on if you can connect the Juice Distributor to the Saucer Section.

Denise There.

Dr Potty That's fantastic. (He pauses.) Do the instructions tell us what to do now?

Denise They say, 'The machine works by attraction. If the machine senses a relic, it will pull the operator towards the relic.'

Dr Potty I understand that.

Denise It also says, 'Warning: If the dial is not tuned in correctly, there may be some side effects when in use! Turn on machine by twisting the dial.'

Dr Potty (Turning on the RD.) Ohh! It's starting!

The noise of a vacuum cleaner can be heard in the background. Suddenly Dr Potty and Denise go potty for 30 seconds – the children join in. Use a suitable backing track for this – laughing and moving around in a very strange way! They click out of it at the end of the 30 second period. This dance can then be used in all the following sketches with the children joining in.

Dr Potty Wow!

Denise It says here that one of the possible side effects is for those close to the machine to go potty for about 30 seconds!

Dr Potty I thought I was potty all the time! Let's try again!

Denise Aaaghh… turn it off!

Dr Potty Why?

Denise (Shouting and rushing off the stage.) Turn it off!

Dr Potty I wonder what side effect that was. (Shouts off-stage.) It's turned off.

Denise (Coming back on.) That's the side effect that makes everyone want to go to the toilet – known as the 'Agh Effect'!

Dr Potty One more try…

Denise Look, Dr Potty, it's pulling you towards the big section of the 'Relic with the Missing Onion Shaped Piece' – it must be working.

Dr Potty Great! The website has provided us with a fantastic device. Mmm, I wonder what we should call it.

Denise Well, if you were to ask me what I think…

Children What do you think, Denise?

Denise Glad you asked me. I think we should name this device, 'The Relic Detector'. Come on, we've got a relic to find! (To audience, in heroic-type voice.) My name is Denise, his name is Dr Potty and that's his Relic Detector!

Dr Potty (To audience, in the same voice.) You've been watching the Adventures of Dr Potty. The search continues tomorrow*, bye! (* State day of next episode.)

Denise and Dr Potty leave.

Dr Potty (Singing.) 'We're finding relics in the morning.'

Denise (Shouting from back stage.) Are we going to visit your gran, then?

DAY 4
DR POTTY AND PRINCESS POTTY'S POT PARLOUR

THEME
Forgiveness

SUMMARY
The setting has now changed. This episode takes place in Princess Potty's Pot Parlour. The room has a big table with a selection of pots on the top of it. Our heroes enter following the pull of the Relic Detector. It leads them, via a slight detour, to the pots on the table. Dr Potty realises that they are ancient pots and they spot a sign which indicates that this is, in fact, Princess Potty's Pot Parlour where she makes herself up to be a beautiful princess. Denise says she wanted to look as beautiful as Princess Potty, so Dr Potty makes her up. Having looked in the mirror she becomes really upset at the ridiculous state she is left in. Dr Potty, realising how clumsy he has been, asks for forgiveness. They discover by looking at one of the pots that they need to go to the 'Tomb of Facial Restoration' to get Denise's face sorted out. That's where they head off to next!

COSTUMES
Denise Normal, everyday clothes
Dr Potty Lab coat and long multicoloured scarf

PROPS
Table with various pots on including: eye liner, blusher, lipstick and eye shadow (in shocking colours, including bright red and black)
Sign: Princess Potty's Pot Parlour
Note: On the side of one pot, there is a message saying, 'For make-up disasters, go to the "Tomb of Facial Restoration"'

SOUND EFFECTS
Low level noise when the Relic Detector is working.

SKETCH
Dr Potty and Denise enter following the lead of the Relic Detector. It leads them towards the oldest member of the holiday club team!

Dr Potty Ooohh!

Denise It's taking us towards that person.

Dr Potty Excuse me, are you an ancient relic?!

Pyramid Leader I don't think so!

Denise Let's try again! (Adjusts dial.) Oh dear I can feel that Potty Effect again. (Dr Potty, Denise and the children do the 30 second potty dance that was introduced in previous sketch.) Thank goodness we've stopped! (Adjusts dial again.)

Denise Oooh… this time it's taking us towards that room over there…

Dr Potty It's leading us to that table. It's stopped.

Denise Where are we?

Dr Potty I think we are here!

Denise I definitely think we are definitely here, because we are not over there!

Dr Potty Of course we're not over there, otherwise there would be here, and here would be over there!

Denise But we're not over there, we're here.

Dr Potty Yes, that's what I said! We're here!

Denise You just said we were over there!

Dr Potty No I didn't! We're here, here, here! Stop confusing me!

Denise Sorry.

Dr Potty I say – look at those pots. Some of them are very old.

Denise They look very precious to me. What's in them?

Dr Potty Lots of red and black liquids. A few brushes. Look there's a sign – what does it say?

Denise (Turning over the sign at the other end of the table.) It says, 'Princess Potty's Pot Parlour'.

Dr Potty This must be my sister's make-up room then!

Denise Really – even with all these ancient pots in here?

Dr Potty She's the Princess you know – she'll have permission to put her make-up in these old, posh pots!

Denise You know what Dr Potty?

Dr Potty What's that Denise?

Denise If you were to ask me what I think…

Children What do you think, Denise?

Denise Glad you asked me. I think, when you and I were at Princess Potty's wedding last weekend, Princess Potty looked like the most beautiful woman in the world!

Dr Potty She was stunning.

Denise Do you think if I had some of her make-up on, then I would be beautiful too?

Dr Potty Denise – you don't need any make-up on. You are beautiful just as you are.

Denise But it would be fun though!

Dr Potty Tell you what, why don't you pretend to be Princess Potty and I'll pretend to be your servant girl.

Denise Great idea. You start over there, and I'll start over here!

Dr Potty Don't start that again!

Denise Sorry, you ready?

Dr Potty Yep.

Denise Action (Starts to pretend to be a bit posh.) Servant, come here please.

Dr Potty (In high pitch voice.) How can I help you your majesty?

Denise I would like you to put my make-up on, please.

Dr Potty I've always wanted to wear some of your make-up Princess! Which colour suits me best? (Goes to put it on himself.)

Denise No, you stupid servant! I'd like you to put make-up on me – to make me look beautiful for my wedding this afternoon!

Dr Potty OK, your majesty. What shall I put on first?

Denise Blusher! (Dr Potty takes the pot of bright red blusher and puts it all over Denise.)

Dr Potty OK!

Denise Next I'd like some eye-liner. (Dr Potty makes a real hash of putting Egyptian style eye-liner on.)

Dr Potty OK!

Denise I'd like some lipstick. (Again, Dr Potty makes a real mess of this.)

Dr Potty OK!

Denise Lastly, a bit of eye shadow. (Dr Potty chooses a ridiculous colour and slaps it on.)

Dr Potty That's it, your majesty.

Denise How do I look?

Dr Potty Beautiful – the most beautiful girl in the whole of Egypt!

Denise Let me look in my mirror. (Picks up mirror and screams! Comes out of character.) Dr Potty, I look HORRIBLE!

Dr Potty I wouldn't say that.

Denise (Starts to cry.) You've made me look ridiculous – everyone is laughing at me. Oh I'm so upset.

Dr Potty Well, I wonder what I did wrong.

Denise Well, if you were to ask me what I think…

Children What do you think, Denise?

Denise Glad you asked me. I think you were clumsy and careless.

Dr Potty Denise, I'm really sorry, I didn't mean to upset you. I've just never put make-up on before! Will you ever forgive me?

Denise (Turning to audience, whilst Dr Potty picks up a pot.) Children should I forgive him, or not?

Children Yes!

Denise OK, Dr Potty, I forgive you. Can you wipe it all off my face now, please?

Dr Potty Oh dear… I've just read the instructions on the outside of this pot!

Denise What does it say?

Dr Potty It says, 'This ink is an almost permanent writing ink. If used by mistake as make-up, you need to go immediately to the "Tomb of Facial Restoration" to get your face sorted out!'

Denise There's no time to lose! Quick, pick up the Relic Detector!

Dr Potty I've got it!

Denise (To audience, in heroic-type voice.) My name is Denise, his name is Dr Potty and that's his Relic Detector!

Dr Potty (To audience, in the same voice.) You've been watching the Adventures of Dr Potty. The search continues tomorrow*, bye! (* State day of next episode.)

Denise and Dr Potty leave.

Dr Potty (Singing.) 'We're making faces in the morning!'

Denise (Shouting from off-stage.) Waaahhh!

DAY 5
DR POTTY AND THE TOMB OF FACIAL RESTORATION

THEME
Reconciliation

SUMMARY
The setting has now changed again to the Tomb of Facial Restoration. Dr Potty and Denise arrive to find it full of amazing objects. They turn on the Relic Detector and find it leads them to a pile of cards for them to read and follow. These, thankfully, are instructions for Facial Restoration. They prove to be very messy! In the end they find that the bottom piece is actually showing some very strange writing, a lot bigger than the others, and doesn't make sense. It is also quite dirty and needs cleaning. Eventually they clean it and realise that it might be the ancient relic they are looking for. They test the cleaned-up piece with the Relic Detector and it proves to be overwhelmingly powerful, confirming the diagnosis. They ring up Mummy, who walks in with the relic. The 'Secret of the Secret Message' is revealed! They all leave very excited and desperate to find Princess Potty.

COSTUMES
Denise Normal, everyday clothes
Dr Potty Lab coat and long multicoloured scarf
Mummy Again dressed up in toilet rolls to look like a mummy

PROPS
Various boxes, tables, chairs and other bits and pieces across the acting area
'Relic with the Missing Onion Shaped Piece'
The pile of 'biscuits' used on Day 2, which today become the cards for Facial Restoration
A low-power water pistol
Can of pie-foam and paper plate
Towel
Child's hanging mobile
Chair

SOUND EFFECTS:
Low level noise when the Relic Detector is working
'Dramatic moment' music

SKETCH
Dr Potty and Denise arrive carrying the Relic Detector.
Dr Potty I think this must be it, Denise.
Denise I hope so Dr Potty!
Dr Potty Morning, children!
Children Morning, Dr Potty!
Dr Potty Oh Denise – your make-up has smudged!
Denise That's because I've been crying so much and trying to hide my face from anyone who comes near me!
Dr Potty (Looking thoughtful.) That pot, which told us to come here, was a very ancient pot. I'm going to turn on the Relic Detector to see if there are any ancient instructions for Facial Restoration.
Denise Can you manage? (Goes to help Dr Potty with the Relic Detector.)
Dr Potty I think so… here we go!
Dr Potty Where is it leading you?
Dr Potty starts moving around the room in a very silly way.
Dr Potty I don't know, but I think I might be having a bit of that Potty Effect! (Everyone does the 30 second potty dance.)
Denise Try adjusting the dial!
Dr Potty There, is that better?
Denise Arrrgh, no!!! (Pretends to need the toilet badly.)
Dr Potty Oh dear! How about that? Ooohhhhhhhhh! (He is suddenly attracted to the pile of cards for Facial Restoration. They are stacked with the relic piece lying at the bottom of the five other pieces.)
Denise That must be them! Let me have a look.
Dr Potty What do they say?
Denise 'These are the instructions for Facial Restoration!'
Dr Potty Right – you read them one by one and I'll do the business! Sit yourself down on this chair!
Denise First wet the face.
Dr Potty (Picking up water pistol and firing it straight at Denise.) What next?
Denise Apply Facial Masking Cream.
Dr Potty picks up pie foam can and paper plate, puts pie foam on plate and puts plate in Denise's face.
Denise Apply more water!
Dr Potty picks up water pistol again and wets Denise for a second time.
Denise Pass the victim the Towel for Final Facial Restoration
Dr Potty There you are.
Denise (Using the towel to wipe off the mess from her face.) Now you have to sing.
Dr Potty 'We're mending faces in the morning. Ding-dong the Tomb is gonna boom!'
Denise There, how do I look?
Dr Potty A lot better! Is that it then?
Denise That's it, except there's this extra card at the bottom here which is rather dirty. Let's clean it a bit – I can't read what it says.

Dr Potty OK, here we go.

They clean it up a bit using the Towel for Final Facial Restoration.

Denise It says – 'arm me ... for the best.'

Dr Potty That's not a very clear instruction.

Denise This piece is a really funny shape. It's in the shape of an onion – how funny!!

Dr Potty The shape of an onion – that is strange!!

Denise and Dr Potty THE SHAPE OF AN ONION!

Denise This could be the missing onion piece from the 'Relic with the Missing Onion Shaped Piece'!

Dr Potty I'll turn the Relic Detector on, to see if it's attracted. Here we go.

As soon as it is turned on, it goes mad and is mega-attracted to the onion shaped piece.

Denise That must be it – turn the machine off.

Dr Potty switches machine off but it still keeps being mega attracted to the piece, Dr Potty continues trying to pull it away from the onion shaped piece, eventually trying to prize it away using his foot, then machine turns off by itself and Dr Potty and Denise both fall over backwards.

Dr Potty Well I wonder what happened there! First it wouldn't switch off and then it turned off on its own.

Denise Well, if you were to ask me what I think…

Children What do you think, Denise?

Denise Glad you asked me. I think we found the relic just in time because the batteries have just run out. We need the rest of the relic!

Dr Potty I think Mummy is at home. I'll give her a ring! (Gets child's hanging mobile out of his pocket and rings up Mummy.) Great news Mummy, I think we've found the missing piece. Please can you bring the 'Relic with the Missing Onion Shaped Piece' to the 'Tomb of Facial Restoration'?

Mummy enters.

Denise Great, she's coming!

Dr Potty Mummy, you are a star! (Gives Mummy a kiss.) Urgh! (Takes relic off her.)

Denise Remind us of what the relic says so far Dr Potty?

Dr Potty It says, 'You tried to h … but God made it turn out'. And now, with the help of this little piece, we will finally know what the message means!

Denise Let me put this missing piece in, to see what it says…

Dramatic sound effect.

Dr Potty It says…

Denise 'You tried to harm me but God made it turn out for the best'.

Dr Potty WOW!

Denise Hold on, that's a bit of the Bible!

Dr Potty Really!?

Denise Yeah, that is exactly what Joseph, the Prime Minister of Egypt, said to his brothers!

Dr Potty There's no time to lose.

Denise We must tell Princess Potty!

Dr Potty Absolutely!

Denise (To audience, in heroic-type voice.) My name is Denise, his name is Dr Potty and that's his Relic Detector!

Dr Potty (To audience, in the same voice.) You've been watching the Adventures of Dr Potty. The search is over, wahey!

Denise, Dr Potty, and Mummy leave in a desperate rush to find Princess Potty.

Dr Potty (Singing.) 'We'll all be famous in the morning!'

Denise (Shouting from off-stage.) Oh yeah!

EPISODE B
DR POTTY AND THE ANCIENT RELIC

Use in Family Service B

THEME

Looking Back!

SUMMARY

Dr Potty and Denise arrive following the directions of the Relic Detector, which directs them to the church leader. Dr Potty asks them if they are an ancient relic, or even Princess Potty in disguise. They decide the settings must be wrong, but go onto recount their adventure to the church leader, and everyone who is in the meeting. They briefly discuss with the church leader the significance of the message on the ancient relic. The sketch ends as Dr Potty and Denise leave to continue their search for Princess Potty.

COSTUMES

Denise Normal, everyday clothes
Dr Potty Lab coat and long multicoloured scarf

PROPS

The Relic Detector
The complete ancient relic

SOUND EFFECTS

Low level noise when the Relic Detector is working

SKETCH

Dr Potty and Denise enter the room carrying the Relic Detector.

Denise What do you mean, you've adjusted the settings?

Dr Potty I changed the settings to help us locate Princess Potty!

Denise That's clever – we haven't seen her all week!

Denise and Dr Potty circle the room in search of Princess Potty, with the Relic Detector finally taking them to the church leader.

Dr Potty Oh, there you are Princess Potty, we've been looking for you everywhere.

Denise Hey, Dr Potty (Whispers to him loudly.) I don't think that's Princess Potty!

Dr Potty Excuse me, are you Princess Potty, or are you someone who is pretending to be Princess Potty?

Church leader I'm not Princess Potty!

Denise (To Dr Potty.) I told you!

Dr Potty (To Denise.) Well, he must be an ancient relic then!

Denise Probably!

Dr Potty Are you an ancient relic!

Church leader I'm the church leader here!

Dr Potty (To Denise.) He is an ancient relic, then!

Denise Oh!

Dr Potty In that case, you might be very interested in what has been happening to us this week!

Church leader I am. In fact we all are!

Denise Hi everyone!

Dr Potty Morning!

Denise Why don't we do a very quick recap on what happened this week for these lovely people, Dr Potty?

Dr Potty (This should be quick and use lots of body language!) OK! Last weekend, it was Princess Potty's wedding to the Egyptian Prince. I was a bit jealous of her, but she asked me to search for the missing piece from the 'Relic with the Missing Onion Shaped Piece'.

Denise Then we met Mari-Anne and she made some lovely onion biscuits to an ancient recipe! This didn't help the search much though!

Dr Potty Denise did find a great idea on the Internet that night, and the following day we built this, the Relic Detector. It helps you to find ancient relics!

Denise Apart from a few side effects, like making you want to go to the toilet…

Dr Potty Or this effect that makes you go Potty (Adjusts the dial and everyone does the 30 second potty dance.)

Denise Apart from those side effects it has helped us enormously! The first ancient relic we found was [name Pyramid Leader who was mentioned on day 3] and then it led us to Princess Potty's Pot Parlour!

Dr Potty Then I made a bit of a mess of Denise's face, trying to make her look like Princess Potty, so we had to go to the Tomb of Facial Restoration.

Denise Yeah, and when we got there, we found out how to make my face look better, and we also found the missing piece to the Relic! And here's the little piece in the big piece! (Holds up relic for everyone to see!)

Dr Potty And do you know what, Mr(s) Church Leader, it's got an amazing message on it!

Church leader What does it say?

Denise Well it says, 'You tried to harm me but God made it turn out for the best.' This is actually a bit of the Bible, where Joseph told his brothers who he was and that God had planned for him to be in Egypt anyway!! This relic is 3,600 years old!

Church leader That's fantastic!

Dr Potty Incredible. Anyway, erm…

Denise If you were to ask me what I think…

Children What do you think Denise?

Denise Glad you asked me. I think if he's not Princess Potty, we must have got the wrong place.

Dr Potty Mmm, and no one else here looks quite pretty enough. I think you're right Denise.

Denise Let's go find her, Dr Potty.

Dr Potty Good thinking, Denise!

Denise (To audience, in heroic type voice.) My name is Denise, his name is Dr Potty, that's his Relic Detector and (Pointing to the church leader.) this is a very ancient relic!

Dr Potty (To audience, in the same voice.) You've been watching the final episode in the Adventures of Dr Potty. The story is over!

Denise and Dr Potty exit following the lead of the Relic Detector.

Dr Potty (Singing.) 'We're getting married in the morning!'

Denise (Shouting from off-stage.) No we're not!

The End

PYRAMID ROCK REGISTRATION FORM (Please use a separate form for each child.)

PYRAMID ROCK will take place at _____ from _____ to _____. Please fill in this form to book a place for your child.

Child's full name		Sex: **M / F**
Date of birth	School	
Please register my child for PYRAMID ROCK	Parent's/Guardian's signature	
Parent's/Guardian's full name		
Address		
Phone number		
I give permission for my child's and my details to be entered on the church database.		**Yes / No**

PYRAMID ROCK CONSENT FORM (Please use a separate form for each child.)

Child's full name	Date of birth
Address	
Emergency contact name	Phone number
GP's name	GP's phone number
Any known allergies or conditions	

I CONFIRM THAT THE ABOVE DETAILS ARE COMPLETE AND CORRECT TO THE BEST OF MY KNOWLEDGE.
In the unlikely event of illness or accident, I give permission for any appropriate first aid to be given by the nominated first-aider. In an emergency, and if I cannot be contacted, I am willing for my child to be given hospital treatment, including anaesthetic if necessary. I understand that every effort will be made to contact me as soon as possible.

Signature of parent/guardian: _____   Date: _____

PARENT/GUARDIAN COLLECTION SLIP

PYRAMID ROCK

CHILD'S NAME

_____

PYRAMID LEADER'S NAME

_____

COLLECTION SLIP

FRONT

Please make sure that you collect this slip when you bring your child each day. You will need it to collect your child at the end of the session. If your child is to be collected by someone else, please pass on this slip to that person.

If you are unable to do this, or if your child is to go home on his/her own, please note this below, and return the slip to the registration desk immediately.

☐ Tick here if your child may go home alone.
☐ Tick here if someone else will collect your child.

Write that person's name next to the day concerned.

MONDAY _____
TUESDAY _____
WEDNESDAY _____
THURSDAY _____
FRIDAY _____

Please sign here if you have ticked either of the boxes above:

_____

Thank you for your cooperation.

PYRAMID ROCK emergency phone number:

REVERSE

If, when dropping off the child, the parent signs the reverse to say that their child may go home alone or with someone else, the registrars should give that slip to the child's Pyramid Leader during the session.

If a person wants to collect a child, but neither they nor the Pyramid Leader has the slip, they should be referred to the Holiday Club Leader, who will make sure that they are authorised to collect the child before allowing them to do so.

EVALUATION FORM

Use this evaluation form to review the session at **PYRAMID ROCK**. Be open and honest about how you felt it went and include any suggestions you have for the next session. Adjust your material on the basis of your discoveries.

THE AIMS
Evaluate the aims for this session. Do you think the club as a whole, and your Pyramid Group in particular, achieved the aims for today? Why was this? Do you need to change anything for the next session?

EGYPTIAN CRAFT AND GAMES
Review these parts of the programme and consider how they fitted in with the rest of the day.
Craft:

Games:

RED HOT!
How did the children react to the Red Hot! time?

THE CHILDREN
Which parts of the programme did the children react best to? Why do you think this was?

Was there anything that was particularly successful?

Think of each child. How did they respond to the teaching? Is there anything you need to do to help a specific child?

Is there anything that needs rethinking?

BIBLE TEACHING AND JOSEPH'S JOTTER
How did the children respond to the Bible teaching, *Joseph's Jotter* activities and discussion you had around the story?

YOU
Identify any areas of the day that you were unhappy with. What problems did you see and what solutions can you offer to the rest of the team?

Did they enjoy it?

Do you have any general comments or suggestions for the next day?

MEGA-GAME
DAY 1

PHOTOCOPIABLE

MEGA-GAME
DAY 2

MEGA-GAME
DAY 3

PHOTOCOPIABLE

MEGA-GAME
DAY 4

MEGA-GAME
DAY 5

PHOTOCOPIABLE

PART 6
IDEAS BANK

UP THE NILE!

This is a 40-minute session to include small-group Bible reading, refreshments and activities. This is an active section that can be run in different ways. After the time in small groups you can move onto craft and/or games.

Either every Pyramid Group does the same activity on the same day:

PROS one simple explanation from the front is needed, and Pyramid Leaders can help each other. It also helps to develop relationships within the Pyramid Groups. Activities can be aimed at specific age groups.

CONS this requires a lot of resources to be used all at one time.

Or sets of activities are set up for the week and children rotate around these activities:

PROS fewer resources are need for each activity, more activities are possible, and different leaders can take responsibility for leading the same activity each day.

CONS it is harder to theme each activity to the day's teaching. Some groups may not have their Pyramid Leader with them during this time if they are leading another activity. You will probably need specific areas which can be dedicated to each activity, and your venue may not be large enough.

EGYPTIAN GAMES

1 BOAT ATTACK

AIM to knock as many cuddly toys as possible off a boat (bench) in five minutes.

EQUIPMENT cuddly toys (see Fun Egyptian Facts on page 56 for some fun ideas), set of beanbags (you might be able to borrow these from a local school), masking tape, table or bench, boat shape cut from paper, which runs the length of the table or bench

Stick the shape of the boat to the bench and place the cuddly toys out along the 'boat'. Mark out a masking tape line about three metres away on the 'shore'. Stand the children behind the line and give them the beanbags. On your signal, the children start to throw the beanbags at the cuddly toys to knock them off the boat. A leader behind the boat returns the beanbags. When all the toys have been knocked off, put the toys back on the boat again and continue the game. Each toy knocked off scores the team a point.

2 NEWSPRINT MUMMIFYING

AIM to design, make and model the best Egyptian mummy

EQUIPMENT newspapers or newsprint (newspaper with no print, which leaves no ink marks – ends of rolls can be obtained from printers for a short fee), sticky tape, scissors, felt-tip pens

Briefly discuss the process of mummification with the children (see Fun Egyptian Facts on page 56). You may wish to show them a few drawings or pictures. Give the children a pile of newspapers and tell them to wrap up one or two group members and decorate them with suitable markings using the felt-tip pens. You will need a large amount of sticky tape for this manic 15 minutes! It would be great to take a picture of each mummy using a digital camera. The results can then be shown to the whole holiday club!

3 PARACHUTE GAMES

AIM to have loads of fun with a multicoloured parachute

EQUIPMENT parachute (you may be able to borrow one from a local school or play centre), soft balls, whistle

There are many different games you could play. Here are a couple of ideas:

Parachute football
Split the children into two teams, who then face each other over the parachute. Two leaders are referees and stand opposite each other in between the teams. Throw a soft ball on to the parachute. A team scores a goal when the ball flies off the parachute over the side of the opposing team. A goal is also conceded if the children handle the ball, although they are allowed to head it.

Crocodiles in the Nile
The children sit around the edge of the parachute with their legs underneath the chute itself. A leader nominates a few children to act as crocodiles, who go under the parachute. The other children must try to roll 'little fish' (soft balls) to one another under the parachute, while the crocodiles try to catch the little fish before they reach the other side. You could play in teams, one rolling the balls and the other being the crocodiles. Time how long it takes each team to catch all the little fish.

4 CAPTAIN KETCHUP'S SUPERHERO GAME
AIM to stay out of Pharoah's pyramid by doing the actions which correspond with the commands shouted out by the leader

EQUIPMENT decorations for the pyramid, such as plastic spiders and snakes, Egyptian masks etc

A small area to the side of the room should be designated Pharoah's pyramid and decorated accordingly. The game leader introduces a list of commands and demonstrates the superhero actions which go with the commands. The children follow each command as quickly as possible. The last child to start doing an action is sent to sit in Pharoah's pyramid. Children should be regularly allowed to join back in the game, eg after each 'Superbunch X' is called. It is worth highlighting the need for sensible and thoughtful play.

Superhero commands and actions
SPIDERMAN Crawl around the room on all 4s
BANANAMAN Bend like a banana
WONDERWOMAN Do a big spin
SUPERMAN Fly around the room, one hand leading the way
BUZZ LIGHTYEAR Shout, 'To infinity and beyond!'
ACTION MAN Move arms up and down (until Bananaman is called)
THERMO MAN Walk around beaming at everybody
BATMAN Fly straight to the front of the room with arms making a bat flap
TARZAN Shout, 'Aaaaagh!' and swing towards the back of the room
SUPERPOSE Pose like a superhero
CAPTAIN KETCHUP Do the Ketchup dance!
SUPERBUNCH X Get into groups of superheroes of a certain number

5 SLAVE-DRIVER
AIM to survive being captured by the ancient Midianites

EQUIPMENT set of hoops (these could be borrowed from a local primary school), music, whistle

Appoint a couple of leaders or children to be 'slave-drivers'. Place the hoops around the room as 'safe houses'. The children dance to the music (maybe gaining extra points for outrageous dancing, if you are using a points system) and avoiding the hoops. When the shout, 'Slave-drivers are coming!' is given, the children run into the safety of the nearest hoop. If a 'slave-driver' manages to tag a child before they reach a hoop, they are 'out'. Gradually, the number of children playing is reduced until you have one or two winners. If you have different colour hoops, you can add an extra shout to warn that some are not safe: 'Slave-drivers are coming, red's not safe!' for example. It is worth talking through with the children the need to be thoughtful and safe as they play.

OTHER GAMES
Some creative thinking around the Egyptian theme may well spark off other fun games. Team relay races using a variety of equipment always go down well. The best games are often the ones where children are able to use up loads of energy whilst having fun.

EGYPTIAN CRAFT
The main purpose of a craft activity time is to allow leaders to get to know the children and talk about their relationship with God whilst doing something practical together. It is tempting to get so involved in ensuring every child finishes their craft that team members can lose sight of this. Remember, it is not important that every child finishes the craft. There will be plenty of time to finish in other Pyramid Group times.

1 HAMA BEAD COASTERS
EQUIPMENT Hama beads, boards (available from most toy shops), iron and ironing paper

Give out boards and boxes of beads to the children. Encourage them to make Egyptian designs by placing the beads carefully on their board. You could provide templates to follow, although the children will probably come up with fantastic designs on their own! Pharaoh's mask, palm trees, pyramids and a sphinx are all possibilities. When their design is complete, they should take the coaster carefully to the leader who is in charge of ironing the beads. (Be very careful when using an iron near children. Set up an area around the iron in which children are not allowed to go.)

2 CAT MASKS

EQUIPMENT simple card cat mask for each child, tissue paper, scissors, elastic, felt-tip pens and other decorative art materials

Using a variety of materials, decorate and colour the mask. Towards the end of the session, staple onto the mask the piece of elastic which will hold the mask to the child's head.

3 CLAY PYRAMIDS

EQUIPMENT quick-drying clay, small pieces of card, small plastic bags

Help the children make small clay bricks which can be built into a clay pyramid. When they have finished, put the pyramid inside a plastic bag with a labelled piece of card, to ensure that bits don't fall off when it is taken home. To create a big pyramid, it may be a good idea to have groups or pairs of children working together.

4 HIEROGLYPHICS

EQUIPMENT bookmarks, T-shirts or other ready-made products onto which the children can draw their names in hieroglyphics and decorate, fabric pens, felt-tip pens, hieroglyphic alphabets (type 'hieroglyphs' into an Internet search engine)

Give the children a bookmark, T-shirt or some other item on which to draw their names. They should then carefully write their names in hieroglyphics and decorate it appropriately to take home.

5 PYRAMID MEMORY VERSE MOBILES

EQUIPMENT outlines of different sized pyramids, pens, glue, wire coat hangers, string, words of memory verses cut out (for younger children).

Give out the pyramid shapes and encourage the children to write one or two words from the memory verse on each one (younger groups can stick on pre-prepared words). Decorate the shapes and tie them to wire coat hangers to create a mobile. Each child could make their own mobile, or you could make one per Pyramid Group.

6 MULTICOLOURED COAT COOKIES OR ONION-SHAPED BISCUITS

EQUIPMENT precooked plain 'shaped' biscuits, decorations (different coloured icing, raisins, chocolate beans etc), plastic food bags

Wash hands, then give the children biscuits to decorate. Invite them to make their biscuits as colourful as possible. The children should take their biscuits home at the end of the day. (Be aware of food allergies. You can get wheat and gluten-free products from many supermarkets, but be sensitive to children who still might not be able to take part.)

FUN EGYPTIAN FACTS

▲ In 1500 BC, a shaved head was the ultimate in feminine beauty. Egyptian women removed every hair from their head with golden tweezers and polished their scalps with buffing cloths.

▲ Both men and women wore make-up.

▲ The base of the Great Pyramid of Cheops could fit about 7 or 8 football pitches. It is made of about 2,300,000 stone blocks, and there are 89 other pyramids in Egypt.

▲ Pyramids would include a toilet.

▲ Most Egyptians died before they were 30.

▲ Egyptians preserved dead bodies of royalty by sealing them with bandages and then coating it with a mixture of wax, oil and salt. The brains were pulled out through the nostrils, the body was washed in fresh water and sweet palm oil.

▲ Mummies were sometimes buried with dolls!

▲ The Egyptians were very religious and believed in lots of gods.

▲ Priests shaved every three days, had three baths a day and wore white linen and sandals. They served for three months in the temple and nine at home.

▲ Pharaoh was known as a god on earth.

▲ In Egypt, cats were sacred and killing a cat was punishable by death. Egyptians shaved their eyebrows to mourn the death of their cats!

▲ Egyptians thought onions kept evil spirits away. When they took an oath (made a promise) they placed one hand on an onion! (As Dr Potty does!)

▲ Egyptian food included cucumbers, celery, lettuce, onions, garlic, leeks and cress. Most lived on bread and onions. They had fruit, including melons, figs, pomegranates and dates, and grapes (which they turned into wine).

▲ The first sweets were made as early as 1600 BC.

▲ Paper was called papyrus – made from reeds laid in a criss-cross pattern, hammered and dried under the sun. Egyptians wrote from right to left.

PART 7
SESSION OUTLINES

PLANNING YOUR SESSION

When you come to plan each day, make sure you have read the descriptions of the programme in Part 1. Select the activities according to the children you are likely to have at the club. Use the evaluation form on page 50 at the end of each session to identify areas that might not be working well and to get ideas on how to change those areas.

YOU DO NOT NEED TO INCLUDE ALL THE ACTIVITIES LISTED HERE IN YOUR PROGRAMME.

MAKING YOUR CHOICE

There are many factors which will influence your choice of activities:

▲ The children involved. The children should be the the most important consideration when choosing the daily activities. Children respond differently to the same activity. Pyramid Leaders in particular should bear this in mind when planning their Up the Nile! time.

▲ The length of the club. Simply, if you have a long club, then you will be able to do more! The timings given are merely guidelines, different children will take different lengths of time to complete the same activity. Be flexible in your timings, judge whether it would be more valuable to complete an activity, even though it may be overrunning, rather than cut it short and go on to the next activity. Have something in your programme you can drop if things overrun.

▲ The leaders available. Not every club will be able to find leaders with the necessary skills to fulfil every requirement. If you can't find anyone with a Basic Food Hygiene Certificate, you will have to limit the refreshments you can provide. If you don't have musicians, then you'll have to rely on backing tracks or miss out the singing. If you don't have anyone dramatic, you might have to miss out the drama.

To help Pyramid Leaders perpare for the Up the Nile! time, the questions for each day can be found in the **PYRAMID ROCK** website.

HELPFUL SYMBOLS

Throughout the book, you will see these two symbols:

ALL TOGETHER
Whenever you see this logo, it means that all the children are together to do these activities.

PYRAMID GROUPS
This logo indicates that these activities are to be done in Pyramid Groups, in each group's Pyramid Pad.

SUNDAY 1

FAMILY SERVICE OUTLINE

A GREAT BIG GOD WITH A GREAT BIG PROMISE

AIMS

▲ To introduce the theme of God's chosen people and reflect on God's great promise to Abraham.

▲ To pray for the leaders of the club and encourage the whole church's involvement, throughout the week.

▲ To encourage children and their families to be part of **PYRAMID ROCK**.

Key story: God's promise to Abraham.

Key link to the holiday club: This story is the background to the story of Joseph. Abraham is Joseph's great-grandfather and Joseph becomes a major player in the fulfilment of this amazing promise.

Key passage: Genesis 15:1–5

SERVICE OUTLINE

INTRODUCTION
The Holiday Club Leader should give the church an overview of the aims and content of the week at **PYRAMID ROCK**. The congregation should be encouraged to support the club through prayer, encouragement and practical help wherever possible.

SONGS
Ask the band, The Cool Cats, to introduce the **PYRAMID ROCK** theme song. (Alternatively, use the song from the DVD.)

THE ADVENTURES OF DR POTTY: DR POTTY AND THE WEDDING
Meet Dr Potty and Denise on their way to a very special wedding! See page 37.

STORY
Introduce Abraham as the man God chose 4,000 years ago to be the founder of God's people. He left his home town to travel to an unknown land, knowing that God would lead him. Abraham was an old man and had no children. How could he be the father of a new nation? Let's read one conversation God had with Abraham in a vision.

Put the story of Genesis 12:1–5 on the screen for everyone to read together.

CAPTAIN KETCHUP
Introduce everyone to Captain Ketchup, who will be reading the news this week!

Captain Ketchup Good Morning, welcome to the Red Hot News Desk. Over the next few days, I will be bringing you up to date – helping you to 'ketch-up' – with all the news from what has been happening to Joseph. Reports are coming in that— Hold on, I've forgotten to do my theme song! (Introduce the congregation to the Ketchup Dance, which will be used each day before Captain Ketchup reads the news!) Play Captain Ketchup's theme song. The Holiday Club Leader should lead the congregation in the Ketchup Dance. Say goodbye to Captain Ketchup and proceed into the teaching.

TEACHING – PART A

Show the congregation an acorn (if you can get hold of one), a small oak tree (or a planted twig) and a picture of a massive oak tree. Talk about how the oak tree starts as a seed (acorn), then grows into a small plant and then develops into a massive, strong, mighty tree.

Discuss with the children what the very small oak tree needs for growth (food, light, warmth, protection). Also discuss what a strong oak tree is good for (beauty, shelter for animals and birds, and food for others, such as acorns!). Say that the oak tree is a very good picture of God's chosen people. God chose Abraham, as shown in the reading, and promised that he would be a mighty nation – like a mighty oak tree. He would be a blessing to all the other nations and his people will be too numerous to count.

Abraham's son, Isaac, had two sons. The younger son, Jacob, then had twelve sons and at least one daughter. This was where Joseph came in. He was one of the twelve sons. It was as though Abraham's family had grown to the size of this very small oak tree. It needed food, warmth, light and protection, and yet God knew that soon there was going to be a massive famine.

JOSEPH MEGA-GAME: STARS!

Before the service, split the seating area into two. Make two sets of 17 stars, with each set of stars numbered from 1 to 17 and each star having the name of one of the 17 members of Jacob's family written on it as big as possible. They are listed in Genesis 46 – Jacob, Leah, Reuben, Simeon, Levi, Judah, Issachar, Zebulun, Dinah; Zilpah, Gad, Asher; Joseph, Benjamin; Bilhah, Dan, Naphtali (Joseph's mother, Rachel, had died giving birth to Benjamin). Use sticky tape to stick the sets of stars underneath the chairs on each side of the room. When the leader says, 'Go!' the members of the congregation need to find all 17 stars on their side of the room (one star per person) and line up in order down their side of the room. The first team to be in order is the winner!

The congregation can see the size of Jacob's family at the beginning of the story of Joseph!

TEACHING – PART B

Keep the winning team standing up. Stand near this team and state that this was the size of Jacob's family at the beginning of the story of Joseph. It was a very small and fragile 'nation' that God promised would one day become as many as the stars in the universe! How was he going to protect this small nation of 17 people? The answer is found in the amazing story of Joseph. Without our hero, and a loving God, this new nation would have died in the seven-year famine. This week we are going to see some of the wonderful things that God did in the story of Joseph.

Share some of the needs for prayer for the holiday club, encouraging the congregation to take time throughout the week to ask how things are going, to do anything practical that requires help, and to particularly watch out for the overall leader and any other key team members. Challenge the congregation: 'God is a God who makes great big promises! Do you believe that he will answer our prayers this week for **PYRAMID ROCK**?' Encourage them to pray for **PYRAMID ROCK** and to spread the word about what's going on to their friends and neighbours.

PRAYER

Pray for the forthcoming holiday club. This could be done in various ways. Ask people to pray in small groups, or ask the team to come to the front of the church to be prayed for. Also pray for any children in the service who will be attending. Their influence upon their friends who come is as important as any adult input.

CREATIVE PRAYER IDEA

As you pray for the club, ask the congregation to write their names on a special 'Welcome to **PYRAMID ROCK** from…' wall poster. Make sure you put the **PYRAMID ROCK** logo in the centre of the poster and take it with you to the holiday club to welcome the children and parents each morning. This will help children who come to **PYRAMID ROCK** understand that the whole church is behind the project.

WORSHIP

Choose songs that the congregation knows, and worship God together.

DAY 1
PLANNER

AIMS
▲ To help the children settle into the club.
▲ To introduce the children to the story of Joseph.

Key story: Introducing Jacob's children and how Joseph was sold into slavery.

Key belief: God is a planner – he made Joseph, and he has made us, with a purpose. He has good plans for our lives.

Key passage: Genesis 37

The world of a child: Many children's understanding of God will be vague. Here is an opportunity to present God as the one who puts us in families. Of course, things sometimes go wrong in families, just like they did in Jacob's family. You may be able to talk about the pain of an unhappy family and bullying in general. Jealousy, another emotion experienced by Joseph's brothers, is also very much part of a child's life today. Yet God was with Joseph and his unhappy brothers.

TEAM PREPARATION
SPIRITUAL PREPARATION
Read together Psalm 139:1–14

1 TALK TOGETHER
Briefly discuss these questions:
▲ What does this psalm say about us and about the children?
▲ In what ways does this psalm give us confidence that God knows about our holiday club?

2 SHARE TOGETHER
Joseph was born into a troubled family. 'Jacob' means 'he struggles', and Jacob had continued to struggle with other men, including his brother Esau. Jacob's name was changed by God to 'Israel', which means 'He struggled with God'. Jacob, although heir to God's promises, was a troubled man, and many of his sons carried his problems (Joseph was a problem too!). Joseph, from a young age, learned about the God of his great-grandfather Abraham – about his mighty promises and his passionate love for his people. Joseph stood out as someone who believed God and displayed that belief and integrity throughout his entire life.

Today, as you introduce the character of Joseph to the children, you should be encouraged – God knows you inside out. He loves you and is asking you to follow him, to trust him for this holiday club and to let him shine though you, just as he did in the life of Joseph.

3 PRAY TOGETHER
▲ Pray for the day's activities.
▲ Pray for the children as they are welcomed.
▲ Pray for the team, that God will give you everything you need to serve him today.

PRACTICAL PREPARATION

Talk through the morning's programme, and make sure everyone is aware of their responsibilities.

Encourage the team to be as welcoming and interactive with the children as possible. Remind them that Jesus said his kingdom was for children and how today you are all going to begin to share this love with the children who come.

Ensure that all the resources are ready for the various activities.

EQUIPMENT CHECKLIST – DAY 1

SECURITY registration forms, badges, pens, team lists
PYRAMID GROUPS badges, pens, Bibles, Joseph's Jotters, Pyramid Sheets, Open the scroll resources, flip-chart paper, marker pens, Pyramid Pieces
MUSIC music for your chosen songs, including the **PYRAMID ROCK** theme song, and other background music
DRAMA costumes and props
CAPTAIN KETCHUP props and pictures
TECHNOLOGY check PA, OHP/data projector and DVD player are working and in focus, check you have all visuals needed on acetate or PowerPoint
ACTIVITIES all equipment needed for games and craft
HOLIDAY CLUB LEADER running order, notes, key word flashcard
CREATIVE PRAYER David's prayer with actions
REFRESHMENTS drinks and biscuits, or other snacks
TEACHING PYRAMID ROCK DVD and/or Simeon costume

PROGRAMME

PYRAMID GROUP WELCOME
(10 MINUTES)

Play some lively music and display the **PYRAMID ROCK** logo to welcome the children as they arrive and are registered. Also, if you made it, display the welcome poster made during Sunday 1. The children are taken to their Pyramid Groups and introduced to their leader(s). Each child should be given their badge. Give each child a sheet of paper and ask the children to write their names on the top. Then ask them to draw pictures of the people in their family, in a kind of family tree. These can then be stuck up next to each team's Pyramid Pad (on the team's pyramid poster, if you have them) as a way of displaying the families represented at **PYRAMID ROCK**. Pyramid Leaders should spend time getting to know the children. The Holiday Club Leader should visit some of the Pyramid Groups to introduce him/herself and chat. Team leaders should keep several name badges with them for late arrivals, as you go RED HOT!

RED HOT!
(45 MINUTES)

HOLIDAY CLUB LEADER WELCOME

Welcome the children to **PYRAMID ROCK**, and explain the structure of the morning and the action-packed plans you have for the rest of the week. Also comment on the pictures of families beginning to be stuck on the pyramid posters – state that you are going to be looking at one particular family today! Remind children of issues related to fire exits and fire drill, plus health and safety details.

KEY WORD

Display the key word, and at the same time display a small flashcard with the key word on it at the front of the room.

Day 1: PLANNER

Ask the children what the word means. (*Someone who knows what needs to be done and makes it happen.*)

Reveal, or write up, the meaning of the key word. State that this is the key word for today and encourage the children to see how it fits into our programme!

BOUNCING BENJAMIN

Ask the leader chosen to be Benjamin for the week to lead the children in an aerobic workout. This session should be made as active and as fun as possible. One of the aims of this is to use up a lot of energy!

JOSEPH MEGA-GAME: THE MAP

The Holiday Club Leader introduces the rules, before the children play today's game, entitled *The map*.

On the map of Israel and Egypt (see page 51 or the website), there are 12 small pictures all connected in some way with today's story. (You may have to point to each picture.) The Holiday Club Leader shows the map for 30 seconds – the children in their Pyramid Groups need to remember all 12. The map is taken away and the groups have 90 seconds to remember as many as possible. The Holiday Club Leader then reveals the pictures, one by one, so the Pyramid Leaders can mark their team's sheets. Award points for correct answers, if you are operating a points system.

THE COOL CATS
Teach the children the **PYRAMID ROCK** theme song chorus, encouraging them to sing the words as best they can. Teach the children the suitably silly dance to go with it (see actions on page 34).

RED HOT NEWS – WITH CAPTAIN KETCHUP
The Holiday Club Leader welcomes the children to the Red Hot Newsroom and asks them to give a warm welcome to Captain Ketchup, who is going to read today's news. As Captain Ketchup reads the news, it would help to have some pictures up on the screen or artefacts so the children can visualise what is happening in the story. For props, you could use a multicoloured coat. Some useful illustrations are found in H*ow to cheat at visual aids*, Pauline Adams (SU) but there are many illustrations of Joseph's story in children's picture books. Everyone should be ready to jump up for the Captain Ketchup dance – spend a minute or two introducing the children to the Ketchup dance and practising it before going live to the news desk.

Captain Ketchup Good morning everyone, and welcome to the Red Hot News Desk – let's do the Ketchup dance! (*Do the Ketchup dance with CK joining in! Then all sit down and focus on CK.*)

This morning we reported the breaking news from Canaan. God had promised a man named Abraham that his descendents, (his children, his children's children, his children's children's children, his children's children's children's child— you get the picture) would be a massive nation.

God said, 'I will make your descendents into a great nation.' (*Show any family-tree visuals you used for the family service.*)

We are pleased to report Abraham's grandson, Jacob, now has a family of 17. Sadly his favourite wife, Rachel, has died, but he still has his favourite son.

We have just received this news. Apparently, Jacob has given his favourite son, Joseph, a fantastic multicoloured robe. (*Show Joseph's coat.*) His brothers don't look too happy about it!

At this point, show Episode One of the **PYRAMID ROCK DVD** and/or continue with Captain Ketchup and the key witness (Simeon) monologue:

KEY WITNESS: SIMEON
Holiday Club Leader Hello, Captain Ketchup. I think those brothers do look a bit mean – maybe they are jealous!?

Captain Ketchup I wouldn't like to be in Joseph's shoes – or his coat!

Holiday Club Leader Have you got anyone in the studio today that can help us understand what happened next?

Captain Ketchup Funny you should ask, cos here comes Simeon!

Simeon stumbles in, as though thrown in through a time machine.

Simeon Oh, hi… Simeon's the name. I'm the second eldest son of Jacob. God made us one big family, 12 brothers and one sister. We should have been a really big, happy family.

Except we weren't happy. One brother, Joseph, made the rest of us mad! The problem was this: our Joseph was my dad's favourite son and Dad didn't just keep his feelings a secret. He showed everyone how much he loved Joseph.

One day, Dad gave Joseph this really, really posh robe. We all had robes – ours were usually short sleeved and quite rough to wear. Joseph's robe was really long, had fantastic colours and was made out of the most beautiful material. This made us feel really jealous. We wanted to be loved by our dad, but it seemed we were only second best.

Then Joseph started having these dreams. He dreamt that he was a star and all of us brothers were stars too but our stars bowed down to his star! He seemed to think that we were going to bow down to him – our big-head little brother! He had a similar dream about wheat. He really did think God was going to make him more important than us. Then, lastly, Joseph started telling Dad about some of the bad things us brothers got up to. We were not just jealous – we were totally mad with him!

One day, all of us brothers, except Joseph and his little brother Benjamin, were out in the desert taking our sheep to find water. It was quite a long way from home and Dad, apparently, got a bit worried about us, so he decided to send Joseph to see if we were OK. As soon as we saw him in the distance we started planning how we could get rid of him forever.

By the time he arrived, we had a plan. We were going to kill him and throw his body into a pit and then pretend that he had been killed by wild animals. Reuben, the eldest, got a bit scared though – he said it would break Dad's heart, so he persuaded us just to throw him into this pit nearby. So that's what we did. Later, however, a bunch of foreign traders, called Ishmaelites, passed by and Judah came up with this bright idea. We could sell Joseph as a slave! It was brilliant – that way we could get some extra dosh and get rid of our really annoying brother at the same time! Suddenly Joseph was gone. We put the money in our pockets, got his precious robe, tore it up and put animal blood all over it. When we got back to Dad, he assumed that Joseph was killed by wild animals! We obviously didn't tell him the truth!

For all we knew Joseph was dead anyway. A 30-day walk across the desert chained to a camel killed a lot of slaves. There was no doubt we felt guilty, I had terrible nightmares afterwards, but at least our brother Joseph was gone for good. He thought he'd be king over us – not much chance now!

CONCLUSION
The holiday club leader thanks Simeon for his story and then reminds the children of the Key Word for the day: PLANNER. What might it mean for Joseph that God was a planner?

UP THE NILE!
(40 MINUTES)

AT THE OASIS (5 MINUTES)
Serve drinks and whatever snacks you have prepared for today in the Pyramid Pads.

OPEN THE SCROLLS (10 MINUTES)
For older children
In your groups, turn to page 7 in *Joseph's Jotter* and add in the words that describe what the brothers thought of Joseph and what he thought of them. Then read Genesis 37:2–8 on pages 16 and 17.

Check out the names of the brothers in the wordsearch/crossword on page 8 and prayer activity on page 9.

If you are not using *Joseph's Jotter*, draw on a piece of flip-chart paper a picture of Joseph on one half of the page and 11 stickmen to represent his brothers on the other half. Ask the children for words to describe the thoughts and the behaviour of the two groups. Then read Genesis 37:2–8 together to check their responses.

(In reading Genesis 37:2–8, you could ask one child to be the narrator, one to be Joseph and two the brothers. Only ask confident readers to do this.)

For younger children
Use the Pyramid Sheets or the flip-chart paper suggestion above.

For all groups, during the session, adapt these questions to your group.
▲ What did the brothers think of Joseph?
▲ What did Joseph think of his brothers?
▲ Why were the brothers jealous of Joseph? Talk about what jealousy is like in families. (Children may talk about trouble with their own brothers and sisters. If so, listen sensitively and, if appropriate, pray for them.)
▲ What did his brothers think was going to happen in the future?
▲ What plans do you think there are for you in the future? (Page 9 in *Joseph's Jotter* will help you talk about this.)
▲ What do we think we will all be doing next week, in one, three or five years' time?
▲ Share what it means to you that God has a plan for your life. You may want to pray for the children as they think about their future.

EGYPTIAN GAMES AND CRAFT (25 MINUTES)
Theme-related games and craft (see pages 54–56).

PYRAMID ROCKS!
(40 MINUTES)

MEGA QUESTION
Show today's mega question: 'What do you plan to do next Saturday?' Get some answers from the children and emphasise the 'plan' aspect of what they say.

TESTIMONY
Ask the mum or dad of a newborn baby to come and talk about their plans for their child so early on in life. They could also share their hopes for their child and their spiritual ambitions. (Encourage them to bring their baby with them if they can!)
Encourage the children that God loves them and has special plans for them too!

THE COOL CATS
Either sing the **PYRAMID ROCK** theme song or introduce another song to the children.

CAPTAIN KETCHUP'S BIN
Welcome Captain Ketchup back and ask him to share some of the contents of his bin! On Day 1, it will be a matter of introducing his bin, with Captain Ketchup sharing a couple of jokes and a picture to whet everyone's appetite for tomorrow! Captain Ketchup should encourage children to bring in their favourite jokes and pictures next time, writing their name and group on their piece of paper, and putting it in Captain Ketchup's bin when they arrive!

MEMORY JOGGER

Ask the children what they can remember of today's programme, including the key word. Then teach the centre section of the memory verse song and show them the actions. You may find it helpful today not to attempt to use music, but to simply ask the children to walk though the actions and words with you. Alternatively, teach them the first part of the verse if you are not using the song.

> The brothers were jealous of Joseph, and sold him as a slave to be taken to Egypt.
> Acts 7:9

THE ADVENTURES OF DR POTTY:
DR POTTY AND THE ULTIMATE CHALLENGE

Introduce the adventures of Dr Potty and Denise. Today they set off on their search for the missing piece of the 'Relic with the Missing Onion Shaped Piece'. See today's script on page 38.

CREATIVE PRAYER

Tell the children that you are going to pray today using a prayer written over 3,000 years ago by the great King David. David talked about how God has made us and he thanked God for the wonderful way we have been made. This is an action prayer. You or another team member will need to make up a suitable set of worshipful actions and then lead the children while the following prayer is read out:

> You have looked deep into my heart, Lord, and you know all about me.
> You know when I am resting or when I am working,
> And from heaven you discover my thoughts.
> You notice everything I do and everywhere I go.
> Before I even speak a word, you know what I will say,
> And with your powerful arm you protect me on every side.
> I can't understand all this! Such wonderful knowledge is far above me,
> You are the one who put me together inside my mother's body,
> And I praise you because of the wonderful way you created me! Amen.
> (Psalm 139:1–6,13,14)

THE COOL CATS

Sing the **PYRAMID ROCK** theme song to finish.

PYRAMID GROUPS
(5 MINUTES)

If you are using this, give each child a Pyramid Piece. Talk about the story so far and what the children think about Joseph, Jacob and what the brothers did. Encourage them to keep the Pyramid Piece safe at home so they can make up the pyramid at the end of the week. Before they leave, make sure that the children have all their belongings and make sure they are collected by the correct adult.

DAY 1

PLANNER

PYRAMID SHEET PHOTOCOPIABLE

Jacob had given Joseph a fine coat to show that he was his favourite son and so Joseph's brothers hated him. (Genesis 37:4)

Colour this picture of Joseph and his brothers. Draw in the mouth of each brother and Joseph. Are the brothers smiling or cross or shouting?

God had a plan for Joseph's life. God knows what you will be doing next week, next month and next year. Thank God that he knows all about us.

DAY 2

HELPER

AIM
▲ To show the children that God is our helper – he is with us and can help us be strong and wise as he helped Joseph when life got tough.

Key story: Joseph in Potiphar's house and in prison.

Key belief: God the Holy Spirit is our helper, both in the good and in the bad times. He is always with us, giving us strength and wisdom.

Key passage: Genesis 39,40

The world of a child: All children are aware of injustice and will feel for Joseph, who was so unfairly treated. But how do we measure whether God is helping us? Some children may feel life is never really going right for them. We live in an age when everyone is very aware of winners and losers. Celebrities are the great success story! This story has a very powerful message, for God is there whatever is happening and helping us see things through his eyes.

For some children, the concept of marital unfaithfulness is quite unknown but to others the reality is all too close! Bear that in mind as you look at what Potiphar's wife desired. The full story has not been included in **Joseph's Jotter**.

TEAM PREPARATION
SPIRITUAL PREPARATION
Read together John 16:5–16

1 TALK TOGETHER
Briefly discuss these questions:
▲ What does Jesus say here about the role of God the Holy Spirit?
▲ How does God the Holy Spirit help us in our lives?

2 SHARE TOGETHER
Joseph grew up knowing that the God who made the heavens and the earth was really close to him, unlike all the other pagan gods around, including those in Egypt. He knew he could rely on God and he knew he could bring all his needs before him.
▲ How did Joseph cope with the horrific rejection of his brothers? God must have worked in Joseph's heart, taking away the bitterness.
▲ How did Joseph cope with the sexual temptation thrown at him by Potiphar's wife? Joseph knew God's presence, his holiness and his strength.
▲ How did Joseph keep the fires of hope burning during his time in prison? God the Holy Spirit would remind him of the promises of old – a promise to prosper Abraham and his family.

Are there issues you need to deal with? Does God need to take away any bitterness and desire for revenge from your heart? Are you being tempted and need God's help? Do you need to hear God speak his words of love and promise into your life today? Spend some time in silent prayer bringing your thoughts before God.

3 PRAY TOGETHER
▲ Pray for the day's activities.
▲ Pray for the children that they will feel really welcome again today.
▲ Pray for any new children that they will feel really comfortable and loved today.

PART 7 · SESSION OUTLINES · DAY 2

▲ Pray for the team, that God the Holy Spirit would give them special words of encouragement for each child in their groups.

PRACTICAL PREPARATION

Talk through the morning's programme, and make sure everyone is aware of their responsibilities.

Encourage the team to be as welcoming and interactive with the children as possible, keeping a close eye out for new children.

Ensure that all the resources are ready for the various activities.

EQUIPMENT CHECKLIST – DAY 2
SECURITY registration forms, badges, pens, team lists
PYRAMID GROUPS badges, pens, Bibles, *Joseph's Jotters*, Pyramid Sheets, Open the scroll resources, small thought bubbles, glue, flip-chart paper, spare paper, Pyramid Pieces.
MUSIC music for your chosen songs, including the **PYRAMID ROCK** theme song, and other background music
DRAMA costumes and props
CAPTAIN KETCHUP props and pictures
TECHNOLOGY check PA, OHP/data projector and DVD player are working and in focus, check you have all visuals needed on acetate or PowerPoint
ACTIVITIES all equipment needed for games and craft
HOLIDAY CLUB LEADER running order, notes, key word flashcard
CREATIVE PRAYER flag or another object to hold up
REFRESHMENTS drinks and biscuits, or other snacks
TEACHING PYRAMID ROCK DVD and/or Potiphar's female servant costume, tray with some bread on it for Joseph in prison

PROGRAMME

PYRAMID GROUP WELCOME
(10 MINUTES)

Play some lively music and display the **PYRAMID ROCK** logo to welcome the children as they arrive and are registered. Make new children especially welcome. The children go to their Pyramid Groups to meet their leader(s). Each child should be given their badge for the day. Challenge the children to remember the section of the memory verse they learned yesterday. Give any children who did not complete their own family poster to go on the team's pyramid the chance to do so if they wish. Otherwise, just have a good chat in your groups!

RED HOT!
(45 MINUTES)

HOLIDAY CLUB LEADER WELCOME
Welcome the children to **PYRAMID ROCK**, and explain the structure of the morning for any children who are new. Ask the groups to nominate someone who can rush to the front and lead the club in the memory verse from yesterday!

KEY WORD
Display the key word and at the same time display a small flashcard with the key word on it at the front of the room.
Day 2: HELPER
Ask the children what the word means. (*Someone who gives us help and assistance*.)

Reveal, or write up, the meaning of the key word. State that this is the key word for today and encourage the children to see how it fits into the programme!

BOUNCING BENJAMIN
Introduce Benjamin, who then leads the children in their morning aerobic workout! Either use the same routine as the previous session, or add in some new exercises. Make sure you keep energy levels high!

JOSEPH MEGA-GAME: EGYPTIAN FOOD!
The Holiday Club Leader introduces the rules, before the children have a go at today's game entitled: *Egyptian food!*

The Holiday Club Leader shows the children the picture of 11 foods (from page 51 or the website) for 45 seconds for the children to memorise as many foods as they can. The Pyramid Groups have 90 seconds in which to write down all 11 pictures. The Holiday Club Leader then reveals the pictures, one by one, with the Pyramid Leaders marking their team's sheets. Award points for correct answers, if you are operating a points system.

THE COOL CATS
Teach the children the first verse of the **PYRAMID ROCK** theme song and sing it along with the chorus. Encourage the children to sing the words as best they can. Teach the actions (see page 34).

RED HOT NEWS – CAPTAIN KETCHUP
The Holiday Club Leader welcomes the children to the Red Hot Newsroom, and asks them to give a warm welcome to Captain Ketchup, who is going to

read today's news. As Captain Ketchup reads the news, it would be helpful to have some pictures or objects to help the children visualise what is happening in the story, such as a large handkerchief as a symbol of Jacob's grief, or use pictures from *How to cheat at visual aids*, Pauline Adams (SU). Everyone should be ready to jump up to do the Captain Ketchup dance.

Captain Ketchup Good morning everyone and welcome to the Red Hot News Desk – let's do the Ketchup dance! (Do the Ketchup dance with CK joining in! Then all sit down and focus on CK.)

There have been further developments this morning in the story of Joseph.

Yesterday, we showed you this exclusive photo of the moment Jacob gave Joseph his multicoloured robe (or) Yesterday, we showed you the very coat that Jacob gave Joseph!

We then heard that Joseph's brothers had become incredibly jealous of Joseph and threw him in a pit.

Apparently it was Judah who suggested selling Joseph to some Ishmaelites.

Jacob is reported to be very upset to hear from his sons that Joseph is dead.

So Joseph has gone into the distance. The question remains – where is he now? We'll let you know when we have some news.

At this point, show Episode Two of the **PYRAMID ROCK DVD** and/or continue with Captain Ketchup and the key witness (Potiphar's servant) monologue:

KEY WITNESS: POTIPHAR'S FEMALE SERVANT

Holiday Club Leader Oh, that's a very good question! Hello Captain Ketchup. Poor Jacob, he's so upset! What happened to Joseph?

Captain Ketchup No news has reached us yet in the studio.

Holiday Club Leader Has anyone arrived in the studio who might know what happened next?

Captain Ketchup Funny you should ask, cos here comes a servant girl from Egypt!

Servant stumbles in, as though thrown in through a time machine.

Servant Oh, hi. Joseph? Yes I remember Joseph.

I'm one of Potiphar's servant girls. Potiphar is the leader of the Guard, in charge of the soldiers – a very important man in Egypt. Joseph was bought by Potiphar and ended up working with me.

Right from the first time I met him, I liked Joseph. He was a foreigner– a Hebrew shepherd – and Egyptians hate shepherds. He must have felt really alone. He was very handsome and he was very thoughtful towards others. Most male slaves can be quite hard and harsh, their language can be terrible and they are always trying to nick things behind their master's back. Joseph wasn't like that.

He started off cleaning floors like me and he did really dirty jobs, but I wasn't surprised when Joseph was given a more important role. It was obvious to anyone that you could trust Joseph. When I asked Joseph one day why he was different from the other slaves, Joseph smiled at me and told me God was with him, and that he just wanted to do the best for his God.

Soon Joseph was my boss! Potiphar put him in charge of the whole household, and when that happened I was really pleased. For many years, Joseph cared for the house, he cared for the slaves and everyone was happy – all except Potiphar's wife.

You see, Potiphar's wife was really keen on Joseph and kept trying to kiss and cuddle him. Every time she got anywhere near Joseph, he used to run away! Joseph knew what she was doing was wrong. Eventually she told this massive lie and said that Joseph had tried to grab her! He was chucked in jail.

The funny thing was that because Potiphar was in charge of all the soldiers, the dungeon was right next to Potiphar's house. I sometimes took food down to the prisoners – it was stinky, damp and dark down there. I didn't like seeing Joseph once again in chains.

Every time I visited him, Joseph greeted me kindly. He was always polite and, although you could see that he was desperate to get out of jail, you could see that he was trusting in his God.

One day, when I was visiting, I overheard Joseph talking with two other prisoners, Pharaoh's baker and cup-bearer. He was helping them understand the meaning of their dreams. Apparently the baker was to die, and the cup-bearer was to go back to working for Pharaoh. When I heard Joseph talking that day, it got me thinking about dreams. I thought maybe God would give Joseph a dream – a dream about his future. Maybe he already had!

Oh, and I nearly forgot to tell you, Joseph got promoted again! Just like Potiphar had, the chief jailer saw that Joseph was a special man. The jailer put him in charge of all the other prisoners! He was really good at it too.

Got to go. Joseph was a top bloke! See ya!

CONCLUSION

The holiday club leader reminds the children about the key word for the day: HELPER. Joseph knew God was with him and he knew God would help him.

UP THE NILE!
(40 MINUTES)

AT THE OASIS (5 MINUTES)
Serve refreshments in Pyramid Groups.

OPEN THE SCROLLS (10 MINUTES)
For older children
For children using *Joseph's Jotter*, turn to page 10 and underline the words in Genesis 39:3,21,23 (on pages 20,21) which say what Joseph did well and what God did for Joseph. Then complete the maze and the prayer about things that are difficult on pages 11,12.

If you are not using *Joseph's Jotter*, or as well as using it, divide a large sheet of paper in two. On one side, draw a simple Joseph outline inside a house. On the other, draw some prison bars and put Joseph behind them. Read Genesis 39:1–6, listening for what life was like for Joseph in Potiphar's house. Write down beside the house, the group's comments about what Joseph did in Potiphar's house.

Explain briefly that Joseph refused to be disrespectful to Potiphar's wife but as a result he was thrown into prison. Read Genesis 39:19–23.
▲ What was life like for Joseph in prison? How did God help him? Write down the group's comments.

For younger children
Use the Pyramid Sheet and decode part of Genesis 39:3. Read Genesis 39:1–6 and listen out for what life was like for Joseph.

For all children
▲ Talk about the ways in which God helped Joseph (eg learn a new language, be a good slave, do the right thing, cope with loneliness and loss).
▲ Talk about what God has done to help you.
▲ Ask the children what ways they would like God to help them and pray about that together.

EGYPTIAN GAMES AND CRAFT (25 MINUTES)
Theme-related games and crafts (see pages 54–56).

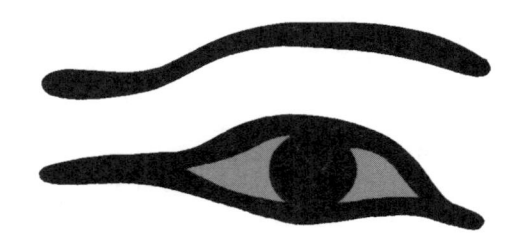

PYRAMID ROCKS!
(40 MINUTES)

MEGA QUESTION
Ask the children today's mega question: 'How do you feel when you are totally alone?' Get a few answers from the children, and from some of the Pyramid Leaders too.

TESTIMONY
Ask one of the team to talk about a time when they were alone, but they were really aware that God was with them, helping them! Remember the points from the training session. It would be good for them to naturally talk about Jesus, who was God on earth. He came alive again and is now with us, helping us.

Encourage the children that God is always with them; he loves them and he offers his special help!

THE COOL CATS
Either sing the **PYRAMID ROCK** theme song or introduce another song to the children.

CAPTAIN KETCHUP'S BIN
Welcome Captain Ketchup back and ask him to share some of the contents of his bin! It is usually helpful if Captain Ketchup gets a few moments during one of the previous activities to look at what children have contributed. He can choose which jokes and pictures are the best to present. This section should be snappy and have pace! You may wish to open up the bin to questions about God, or about CK himself, eg, 'Have you got a girlfriend?'!

MEMORY JOGGER
Ask the children what they can remember of today's programme, including the key word. If you are using the memory verse song, teach the children the last part of the song, together with the actions (see page 33). Join it with the middle section covered on Day 1.

If you are not using the song, use a creative way of learning the second part of verse 9 and the beginning of verse 10:

But God was with him and rescued him from all his troubles.
Acts 7:10

THE ADVENTURES OF DR POTTY: DR POTTY AND THE ONION BISCUITS

Introduce the continued adventures of Dr Potty and Denise. Today they meet a French chef and think they've found the missing piece! See page 40.

CREATIVE PRAYER

Encourage the children that there are loads of amazing things to know about God. He made each one of us and has a plan for us, he is with us all the time and can hear everyone talking at the same time! Tell the children that you are going to pray together today. Ask one leader to wave a flag, or some other object they can hold up easily at the right moment. The Holiday Club Leader (or another leader) reads the simple prayer outlined below. Every time the flag is raised, the children shout their name to God! Don't read the prayer too slowly.

> Dear Lord, it's [flag] here. Thank you that I [flag] could come to **PYRAMID ROCK** today. Thank you for all the fun that I [flag] have had. Thank you that you made me [flag]. Thank you that you are with me, [flag], all the time and thank you that you know my name, [flag]. Please help me [flag] learn loads, and have a great time tomorrow too. Amen

THE COOL CATS

Sing the **PYRAMID ROCK** theme song to finish.

PYRAMID GROUPS
(5 MINUTES)

If you are using this, give each child the next Pyramid Piece. Talk about the story so far and what the children think about Potiphar and how Joseph trusted God, even when he was in prison. Encourage them to keep all the Pyramid Pieces safe at home, so they can make up the pyramid at the end of the week. Before they leave, make sure that the children have all their belongings and make sure they are collected by the correct adult.

DAY 2

HELPER

PYRAMID SHEET PHOTOCOPIABLE

Joseph lived in the home of Potiphar, his Egyptian owner. Soon Potiphar realised that…

Use the code to work out what Potiphar realised!

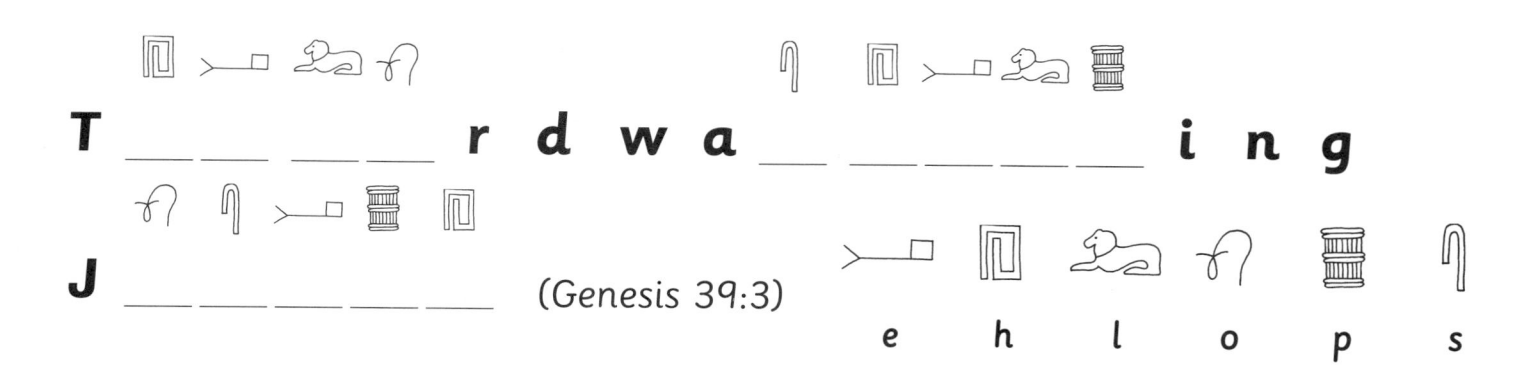

T _ _ _ r d w a _ _ _ i n g
J _ _ _ _ _ _ _   (Genesis 39:3)

e   h   l   o   p   s

Joseph needed God to help him. How did God help him?

Write or draw what you find difficult. Ask God to help you.

DAY 3

PROVIDER

AIMS

▲ To tell the story of how Joseph interpreted Pharaoh's dream and how Joseph was given the job to provide for the nations.

▲ To show that God loves, cares and provides for all he has made, which includes us.

Key story: Joseph interprets the dreams of Pharaoh and provides food for the nations.

Key belief: We can trust God to provide for everything we need – this includes food, favour and wisdom!

Key passage: Genesis 41

The world of a child: Some children will have heard that God is love but it may not make much sense. What is more, adults around them may have questioned how God can exist or care for us in a world of disasters. We need to remember that this is the home background of many children. We should strive to show them the truth: that God does care in practical ways, such as the care the children experience at the holiday club.

TEAM PREPARATION

SPIRITUAL PREPARATION

Read together Matthew 6:25–34

1 TALK TOGETHER

Briefly discuss these questions:
▲ What does Jesus say about God the provider?
▲ Why did Jesus say we should not worry?
▲ On a piece of flip-chart paper make a list of all the things that God provides for us!

2 SHARE TOGETHER

It must have been an amazing day for Joseph. One morning he woke up in prison – a forgotten man. Then before he knew it, he was standing before Pharaoh and listening to his dream. With the help of his heavenly Father, Joseph gave Pharaoh the interpretation for his dream and was immediately promoted to Prime Minister! That must have been some day!

Have you ever felt, 'Where is God when I need him?' Joseph had more cause than most to despair because he was falsely put in prison and abandoned. Yet Joseph knew that God was the great provider. He had always been with Joseph, helping him and blessing him. It could have been, in the darkness of the prison cell, that God began to pour his grace into Joseph's life, enabling him to cope with the bitter rejection by his brothers, and to forgive them.

The story of Joseph encourages us that God knows every situation and he will provide for all we need. God chose Joseph, a man of integrity, to be the Prime Minister in Egypt and to help save the nations.

God still uses people today to provide for others. Who is God asking you to provide for in your everyday life? What is he asking you to do today?

3 PRAY TOGETHER
▲ Thank God for all the wonderful things he provides for us every day. Be specific.
▲ Pray for the day's activities.
▲ Pray for the children that the teaching will really sink in and that they will understand how God provides for them.
▲ Pray as a team that you will shine for Jesus today.

PRACTICAL PREPARATIONS
Talk through the session's programme, and make sure everyone is aware of their responsibilities.

Encourage the team to be as welcoming and interactive with the children as possible. Ask them to make sure that they speak some encouraging words to every child in their group.

Ensure that all the resources are ready for the various activities.

EQUIPMENT CHECKLIST – DAY 3
SECURITY registration forms, badges, pens, team lists
PYRAMID GROUPS badges, pens, Bibles, *Joseph's Jotters*, Pyramid Sheets, Open the scroll resources, A5 paper, glue, flip-chart paper, spare paper, marker pens, Pyramid Pieces
MUSIC music for your chosen songs, including the **PYRAMID ROCK** theme song, and other background music
DRAMA costumes and props
TECHNOLOGY check PA, OHP/data projector and DVD player are working and in focus, check you have all visuals needed on acetate or PowerPoint
ACTIVITIES all equipment needed for games and craft
HOLIDAY CLUB LEADER running order, notes and key word flashcard
CREATIVE PRAYER small pieces of paper, one per child, and a sheet of flip-chart paper
REFRESHMENTS drinks and biscuits, or other snacks
TEACHING PYRAMID ROCK DVD and/or cup-bearer costume

PROGRAMME

PYRAMID GROUP WELCOME
(10 MINUTES)

Play some lively music and display the **PYRAMID ROCK** logo to welcome the children as they arrive and are registered. Each child should be given their badge for the day. Challenge the children to say the memory verse to their Pyramid Leader. Leaders should spend time chatting with the children about what they have done since the last session and discover what they have enjoyed so far at **PYRAMID ROCK**. The Holiday Club Leader should visit some of the Pyramid Groups to say a special hello and chat.

RED HOT!
(45 MINUTES)

HOLIDAY CLUB LEADER WELCOME
Ask some confident children to come to the front and speak out or sing the memory verse with actions. Say that today we are going to see how God rescued Joseph from all his troubles!

KEY WORD
Display the key word, and at the same time display a small flashcard with the key word on it at the front of the room.

Day 3: PROVIDER
Ask the children what the word means. (*Someone who prepares, gives and equips.*)

Reveal, or write up, the meaning of the key word. State that this is the key word for today and encourage the children to see how it fits into our programme!

BOUNCING BENJAMIN
Introduce Benjamin, who then leads the children in their morning aerobic workout! Introduce new exercises today to keep the children's interest.

JOSEPH MEGA-GAME: PYRAMIDS!
The Holiday Club Leader introduces the rules, before the children have a go at today's game, entitled *Pyramids!*

The Holiday Club Leader will show the children a grid of 16 pyramids in eight pairs (see page 52 or the **PYRAMID ROCK** website for a colour version). The teams will need a piece of flip-chart paper prepared with the same empty grid, so that they can write down the pairs of the pyramids in the correct box. The Holiday Club Leader shows the grid for 45 seconds. After the grid is taken away, the children have 60 seconds to tell their Pyramid Leader where the pairs are for the leader to write in the correct grid space. The Holiday Club Leader then gives the children an extra 10–15 second burst of the grid to help the groups that are struggling. The Holiday Club Leader then reveals the grid, with the Pyramid Leaders marking their team's sheets. Award points for correct answers, if you are operating a points system.

THE COOL CATS

Teach the children the rest of the **PYRAMID ROCK** theme song. Add some suitable actions for the second verse. Sing one or two other songs if you wish.

RED HOT NEWS – WITH CAPTAIN KETCHUP

The Holiday Club Leader welcomes the children to the Red Hot Newsroom, and asks them to give a warm welcome to Captain Ketchup, who is going to read today's news. Everyone should also be ready to jump up and do the Captain Ketchup dance at the appropriate moment. You could use some chains as artefacts when talking about Joseph in prison. Use additional pictures for the news from books such as *How to cheat at visual aids*, Pauline Adams, (SU).

Captain Ketchup Good morning everyone and welcome to the Red Hot News Desk – let's do the Ketchup dance! (Do the Ketchup dance with CK joining in! Then all sit down and focus on CK.)

There have been even more developments in the story of Joseph.

As you will remember, Joseph was sold as a slave by his brothers and taken to Egypt.

Joseph was sold to Potiphar, the leader of the Guard. He was responsible for all the soldiers and the prison. Joseph soon became his top slave!

Potiphar's wife then told a massive lie and Joseph was thrown in jail.

In jail, God was still with Joseph and helping him. God helped him become the top prisoner. He even ended up telling the Pharaoh's cup-bearer and the baker, who were in prison with him, the meaning of their dreams.

Was Joseph going to stay in prison for the rest of his life? Was he going to be forgotten forever?

At this point, either show Episode Three of the **PYRAMID ROCK DVD** and/or continue with Captain Ketchup and the key witness (cup-bearer) monologue:

KEY WITNESS: CUP-BEARER

Holiday Club Leader Hello Captain Ketchup. I wonder what it must have been like for Joseph in prison?
Captain Ketchup I think God was looking after him!
Holiday Club Leader I agree. But did he stay in prison for ever? I don't suppose you've got another one of your expert witnesses in the studio have you?!
Captain Ketchup Funny you should ask, cos here comes the Pharaoh's cup-bearer!

The cup-bearer stumbles in, as though thrown in through a time machine.

Cup-bearer Good morning! I am the cup-bearer to Pharaoh, the King of Egypt, his personal servant. I have to taste everything that is given to the king to eat and drink in case someone tries to poison him! It's an adventurous job!

I first got to know Joseph in prison. He was a good man, gentle, forgiving, and he was just brilliant at looking after the prisoners. I couldn't quite work out why such a good man was in prison. Anyway, Pharaoh's baker and I also happened to be in prison – a little disagreement with Pharaoh, if you know what I mean!

One day, something very strange happened. The baker and I both had dreams. When Joseph asked why I was so upset, I told him. He said that God would help him understand what my dream meant, so I told him my dream. He said, 'In three days you'll be back serving wine to Pharaoh!' And do you know what? Three days later I was released and I was back serving the king!

The bad thing was – I forgot all about Joseph. He did say to me, 'Please tell the king about me!' but I just forgot.

Then one day, about two years later, Pharaoh woke up and was really upset. When I tried to give him his morning cuppa, he had tears in his eyes. Before I knew what was happening, lots of important people arrived and Pharaoh told them his dreams. None of them knew what the dreams meant. Pharaoh was really unhappy. It was only then that I remembered about Joseph. I told the king straight away and he sent me to get Joseph from prison.

Joseph looked a wreck, so I gave him a shave and gave him a quick shower (he was really smelly!), and dressed him in some decent clothes. I said sorry for forgetting him and then brought him to the king!

When Pharaoh asked Joseph if he could interpret dreams, he said, 'No!' I couldn't believe it! Then he said that, because God would help him, the answer was actually, 'Yes!' Pharaoh told Joseph that he'd seen seven fat cows come out of the Nile, then seven really skinny ones come out. The skinny ones started to eat the fat ones! He then said that he'd seen seven big bits of grain grow up, then seven thin bits grow up. Again the thin bits of grain ate up the big bits!

Joseph stood there for a moment (I reckon he was praying!) and then he said, 'Pharaoh, these dreams mean the same thing. They are both from God and he's telling you that in the next seven years there will be loads of food. Then the seven years after that there will be no food. There will be a massive famine!' Joseph told Pharaoh that he needed to find someone who could organise the storing of food during the time when there was plenty.

Pharaoh stood there for a moment looking at Joseph, and then he announced to everyone, 'Who can possibly handle this better than Joseph, since he has the Spirit of God inside him?' Suddenly, Joseph went from being a prisoner to being Prime Minister – incredible! He got some posh clothes, Pharaoh's ring, a magnificent chariot and even a new wife!

You know, Joseph was brilliant at his new job. His God really helped him organise the people! We did have seven years with loads of food and Joseph stored loads of grain for the bad years. Then when the bad years came, we were all OK! The other countries around us were in big trouble mind, but we had the food we needed, thanks to my mate Joseph.

Got to go! Bye!

CONCLUSION

The Holiday Club Leader reminds the children about the key word for the day: PROVIDER. Ask the children to think about God providing, when they go into their Pyramid Groups.

UP THE NILE!
(40 MINUTES)

AT THE OASIS (5 MINUTES)
Serve drinks and refreshments. You might want to introduce something celebratory, since Joseph is out of prison and God provided seven years with plenty of food.

OPEN THE SCROLLS! (10 MINUTES)
For older children
If you are using *Joseph's Jotter*, turn to page 27. Read out Genesis 41:50–52 and ask the children to work out hand or body signs for the names of Joseph's two sons: eg 'forget' might be flicking a hand across the forehead, 'troubles' might be pretend crying. Then read verses 53–57 and complete the missing words on pages 14 and 15, thanking God for his care.

If you are not using the *Joseph's Jotter*, write the sentence below on a piece of flip-chart paper and ask the children to choose to be either Joseph, Pharaoh, or the people of Egypt. Read Genesis 41:50–57, using the hand signs as suggested above, and then ask the children to fill in the sentence depending upon who they are.

> Because God cares for me [name],
>   He has provided me with _____

Then ask them to fill in the sentence again as though they are doing it for themselves. Discuss what they say.

For younger children
Read out Genesis 41:54,56 from the Pyramid Sheet. Together work out signs that explain these verses, eg rubbing empty stomachs, sad faces.

For all children
▲ Talk about the things that God provided for Joseph. (Understanding of the dreams, wisdom, a wife and children.)
▲ What did God provide the king of Egypt with? (Warning of the famine, someone who could save them, seven years with loads of food to eat.)
▲ Talk about things we need (not just what we want).
▲ How does God provide for us? You could eat something special in your groups for which you can say a special prayer of thanks to God. (Be aware of any allergies.)

EGYPTIAN GAMES AND CRAFTS (25 MINUTES)
Theme-related games and crafts (see page 54–56).

PYRAMID ROCKS!
(40 MINUTES)

MEGA QUESTION
Show today's mega question: 'What do your parents provide for you at home?' This should not just be objects but more abstract things such as love and protection.

TESTIMONY
Ask a team member to talk briefly about how God has provided for them.

Encourage the children that God continues to provide for them, often through other people, such as parents and friends. God has given Jesus to be their special friend. Pyramid Leaders could contribute from the discussions they had in their Pyramid Groups.

THE COOL CATS
Either sing the **PYRAMID ROCK** theme song or another song with the children.

CAPTAIN KETCHUP'S BIN
Welcome Captain Ketchup back and ask him to share some of the contents of his bin! Captain Ketchup should choose a selection of the pictures, jokes and questions that the children have put in his

bin. Encourage the children to bring in more jokes etc for tomorrow and to make sure they write their name and group on their piece of paper before they pop it in the bin!

MEMORY JOGGER
Ask the children what they can remember of today's programme, including the key word.

If you are using the memory verse song, you should add the reference (the first part of the song) to the memory verse sections. Teach the reference to the children and show them the actions. See if you can put the whole memory verse song together. You may wish to explain that this is a quote from the New Testament. Stephen is speaking to the Jewish leaders about the heroes of the Jewish faith!
If you are not using the song, use a creative way of revising the whole verse (see page 33).

> Joseph's brothers were jealous of him and sold him as a slave to be taken to Egypt. But God was with him and rescued him from all his troubles.
> Acts 7:9,10

THE ADVENTURES OF DR POTTY:
DR POTTY AND THE ONION DETECTOR
Introduce the continuing adventures of Dr Potty and Denise. Denise discovers a relic detector that will help in their search for the missing piece! See today's script on page 41.

CREATIVE PRAYER
Tell the children that Jesus encouraged his followers to talk to God and to ask God for the things they needed. Jesus himself said in Matthew 6:8: 'Your Father (God) knows what you need before you ask him!' But he still loves being asked! Tell the children that they will all be given a small coloured piece of paper. On it they should write or draw something that they would like God to provide for them or their family. They can write down other things apart from possessions, eg happiness, peace inside. They don't need to put their name on it. The small pieces should be stuck on a piece of flip-chart paper by each pyramid group and made into a prayer poster to be stuck up by the team's Pyramid Pad.

THE COOL CATS
Sing the **PYRAMID ROCK** theme song to finish.

PYRAMID GROUPS
(5 MINUTES)

If you are using this, give each child the next Pyramid Piece. Talk about the story so far and what the children think about what happened to Joseph in prison and in front of Pharaoh. Encourage them to keep all three Pyramid Pieces safe at home, so they can make up the pyramid at the end of the week. Before they leave, make sure that the children have all their belongings and make sure they are collected by the correct adult.

DAY 3

PROVIDER

PYRAMID SHEET
PHOTOCOPIABLE

The famine began just as Joseph had said. There was not enough food in other countries but all over Egypt there was plenty... Joseph opened the storehouses and sold the grain to the Egyptians. (Genesis 41:54,56)

Spot nine differences between these two pictures of Joseph selling grain.

God planned for Joseph to go to Egypt. God planned that Joseph would store the food to sell when no grain was growing in the fields.

God showed he cared for people. God provided for them.

Draw something good that God has given you. (It could be someone who cares for you, a pet, something you enjoy, your favourite food.)

Thank God that he cares for you.

DAY 4

FORGIVER

AIMS

▲ To tell the story of how Joseph forgave his brothers when they came to Egypt for food.
▲ To show that God is the forgiver and he still forgives us through the death of Jesus.

Key story: Joseph's brothers come to Egypt for food. Joseph forgives the repentant brothers.

Key belief: Forgiveness is at the heart of having a relationship with God. This is only possible because of Jesus' death. God loves to forgive. Joseph was like his God – he forgave people who had wronged him!

Key passage: Genesis 42:1 – 45:24

The world of a child: Children's awareness of wrongdoing and the need to take responsibility for wrong develops as they mature. All children would recognise that what the brothers did was very wrong, but they may not make any connection with what they do that is wrong. Their awareness of sin separating them from God will also vary with age and experience. Be careful that the language you use to describe sin makes sense to children and is truthful. Do not assume that children know much about the death of Jesus or its meaning.

TEAM PREPARATION

SPIRITUAL PREPARATION
Read together Matthew 26:26–30

1 TALK TOGETHER
Briefly discuss this question:
▲ What does this story tell us about a forgiving God? If appropriate, take some bread and wine and share them together in an informal way, just as Jesus encouraged us to do. Thank him for the forgiveness he has now given to each one of us!

2 SHARE TOGETHER
Forgiveness costs. Evil deserves punishment and, as Paul points out in Romans 3:23, 'All have sinned and fallen short of God's glory.' Each one of us has gone our own way and deserves to be punished by God. But God, in his great mercy, sent his only Son to be our Saviour. His death means that we can be forgiven, once and for all. It is, as the song says, amazing grace! Love we don't deserve. And it cost God his Son.

There is no way that Joseph could have forgiven his brothers if God had not helped him in it. His natural reaction, like anyone's would be, would have been for revenge and to harm those who harmed him. God had been at work in Joseph's life, healing the hurts of rejection – to such a point that he could say to his brothers in Genesis 45:5: 'Don't worry or blame yourselves for what you did. God is the one who sent me ahead of you to save lives.' That's grace! Joseph saw things from God's perspective and he could see why God allowed events to unfurl in the way they did.

Jesus said that if we expect God to forgive us, we need to forgive others (Matthew 6:15). Are there people you need to forgive? Are you carrying painful experiences of rejection which you need God's help with? Ask God to help you with these things.

PART 7 · SESSION OUTLINES · **DAY 4**

3 PRAY TOGETHER
- ▲ Thank God for the fact that Jesus died to make it possible for us to be forgiven.
- ▲ Thank God that his Spirit enables us to forgive others.
- ▲ Pray for the day's activities.
- ▲ Pray that the children will understand what it means to be forgiven by God.
- ▲ Pray that God will give you a real sensitivity to his Holy Spirit as a team, as you minister to the children today.

PRACTICAL PREPARATIONS

Talk through the morning's programme, and make sure everyone is aware of their responsibilities.

Encourage the team to give 100 per cent again this morning and to really enjoy the opportunity to serve the children. Encourage them to chat to parents as they come and go, if appropriate, and to continue to build good relationships with the children.

Ensure that all the resources are ready for the various activities.

EQUIPMENT CHECKLIST – DAY 4
SECURITY registration forms, badges, pens, team lists
PYRAMID GROUPS badges, pens, Bibles, *Joseph's Jotters*, Pyramid Sheets, Open the scroll resources, flip-chart paper, spare paper, Pyramid Pieces
MUSIC music for your chosen songs, including the **PYRAMID ROCK** theme song, and other background music
DRAMA costumes and props
TECHNOLOGY check PA, OHP/data projector and DVD player are working and in focus, check you have all visuals needed on acetate or PowerPoint
ACTIVITIES all equipment needed for games and craft
HOLIDAY CLUB LEADER running order, notes and key word flashcard, copies of *Friends with Jesus* etc to explain God's forgiveness to children
CREATIVE PRAYER small cards with the number 4 written on, or cut into the shape of a 4 (enough for two per child), buckets numbered 1 and 2 (have more buckets if you have a large number of children)
REFRESHMENTS drinks and biscuits, or other snacks
TEACHING PYRAMID ROCK DVD and/or Judah costume

Have booklets ready to help any child who wishes to know more about what it means to be forgiven. See the inside front cover for appropriate SU booklets.

PROGRAMME

PYRAMID GROUP WELCOME
(10 MINUTES)

Play some lively music and display the **PYRAMID ROCK** logo to welcome the children as they arrive and are registered. Each child should be given their badge for the day. Challenge the children to remember the entire memory verse (song) and to say (sing) it to their Pyramid Leaders. Pyramid Leaders should check how the pyramids are going at home, encouraging the children to bring them back to the family service/party at the end of the week. Encourage the children to put their contributions into Captain Ketchup's bin!

RED HOT!
(50 MINUTES)

HOLIDAY CLUB LEADER WELCOME
Ask some confident children to come to the front and perform (with actions) the whole memory verse song, or to say the whole verse. Say that today we are going to see how Joseph did something really amazing!

KEY WORD
Display the key word, and at the same time display a small flashcard with the key word on it at the front of the room.

Day 4: FORGIVER
Ask the children what the word means. (*Someone who forgives or pardons. One who no longer blames!*)

Reveal, or write up, the meaning of the key word. Say that this is the key word for today and encourage the children to see how it fits into our programme!

BOUNCING BENJAMIN
Introduce Benjamin to lead the aerobic work-out. Try to run a theme through the song, such as do everything in groups of 4 (ie 4giveness!)

JOSEPH MEGA-GAME: BROTHERS!
The Holiday Club Leader introduces the rules, before the children have a go at today's game entitled *Brothers*!

Before showing today's picture of some of the brothers asking Joseph for food (see page 52 or the **PYRAMID ROCK** website), the Holiday Club Leader asks the children a series of questions, including:

'How many brothers were kneeling down at Joseph's feet?' The Holiday Club Leader shows the children the picture of for 30 seconds. The Pyramid Groups have 90 seconds to answer all the questions. The Holiday Club Leader then reveals the answers, together with the picture, and the Pyramid Leaders mark their team's sheets. Award points for correct answers, if you are operating a points system.

Some suggested questions might be:
How many brothers kneeled before Joseph?
What was Joseph doing with both his hands?
What was in the corner of the picture?
How many of the brothers had beards?
What shapes are there on the pillar?

THE COOL CATS
Sing the **PYRAMID ROCK** theme song.

RED HOT NEWS – WITH CAPTAIN KETCHUP
The Holiday Club Leader welcomes the children to the Red Hot Newsroom, and asks them to give a warm welcome to Captain Ketchup, who is going to read today's news. Everyone should be ready to jump up and do the Captain Ketchup dance at the appropriate moment. For artefacts, you could have a chain of office and some grain. Additional news pictures could be found in books such as *How to cheat at visual aids*, Pauline Adams (SU).

Captain Ketchup Good morning and welcome to the Red Hot News Desk – let's do the Ketchup dance! (Do the Ketchup dance with CK joining in! All sit down and focus on CK.) There seems to be no end to the dramatic story of Joseph. Here's the story so far!
  Joseph was sold as a slave by his brothers and taken to Egypt.
  Joseph was sold to Potiphar, the leader of the Guard.
  Joseph then ended up in prison for a few years, until…
  Pharaoh had a dream which no one could interpret. Joseph, with God's help, told Pharaoh what the dream meant.
  Pharaoh amazingly promoted Joseph from slave and prisoner, to Prime Minister of Egypt!
  What was going to happen next? What about his brothers? The famine is really bad in Canaan and there are rumours that the brothers have gone to Egypt!
  At this point, show episode four of the **PYRAMID ROCK DVD** and/or continue with Captain Ketchup and the key witness (Judah) monologue:

KEY WITNESS: JUDAH
Holiday Club Leader Oh my goodness, hello Captain Ketchup. Did you say that Joseph's brothers are on their way to Egypt!?
Captain Ketchup The famine is really bad in Canaan where they live. They are getting hungry!
Holiday Club Leader In lots of ways they deserve everything they get because they were so mean to Joseph, but I wonder how Joseph reacted when the brothers did turn up. I don't suppose you've got another one of your expert witnesses in the studio have you?!
Captain Ketchup Funny you should ask, cos here comes Judah, Joseph's brother!
Judah stumbles in, as though thrown in through a time machine.
Judah All of us brothers had nightmares about Joseph. It was I, Judah, who had come up with this 'brilliant' plan to sell him as a slave. What a way to treat your brother! We were so jealous and mad with Joseph. We didn't talk to our father, or to God, we just sold him as a slave to die! The nightmares were terrible.
  Twenty years after Joseph had gone, Benjamin, our youngest brother, wasn't a small boy any more – he was a married man. But now there was a new nightmare – famine! All our crops had failed. Within two years we were starving.
  Jacob, our really old dad, heard that there was food in Egypt, so he sent all of us brothers, except Benjamin, to Egypt. When we got there it was like a different world. We were farmers who lived in tents. In Egypt there were fantastic buildings and a mighty river – it was an amazing place. We were told to go to the Prime Minister for food. We fell on our knees before him and pleaded for food, in exchange for the gold in our bags.
  The Prime Minister, who spoke in Egyptian, accused us of being spies! It was not true! He asked us about our family, about our dad and about our little brother. He wanted to know so much. It was really scary. In the end we left. We had food, but we had to leave our brother Simeon behind in prison, until we brought our youngest, precious brother to Egypt. Our dad was really unhappy when we got back, especially when we told him that the gold we had used to pay for the food had been put back in our bags! The authorities in Egypt would think we were thieves! Dad refused to let Benjamin go back with us to Egypt. He was the only other son of his favourite wife, Rachel. If he were to be killed, like Joseph, I'm sure my dad would die. So Simeon stayed in prison, in Egypt.

The famine got worse and worse. Before long Dad told us we had no choice but to go back to Egypt for more food. I told him that there was no point in going without taking Benjamin, but Dad refused to send him. Eventually we were absolutely desperate, so with tears in his eyes, he let Benjamin go with us. I took personal responsibility for Benjamin's life.

When we arrived, the Prime Minister acted very strangely. We were terrified of him. He fed us (somehow managing to sit us all in age order!) and he gave us food for the journey home. Our money was returned again, but then, after a day's travelling, tragedy struck. An Egyptian soldier tracked us down and found the Prime Minister's cup in Benjamin's bag. He was accused of stealing, we were all marched back to Egypt and Benjamin was chucked in jail.

I fell on my knees, my brothers behind me, asking for mercy. You see, we knew that the trouble we were all in was a punishment from God for what we had done to Joseph. We wished we hadn't sold him. We were changed men – we cared now and there was absolutely no way I was going to break my father's heart and leave Benjamin here! I pleaded with him. I told him I was responsible – put me in prison instead!

And then, the most amazing thing happened. The Prime Minister got everyone to leave the room, except him and us. Then he spoke to us in Hebrew. He said, 'Brothers it's me – your brother Joseph.' A chill went down my spine. In a flash, millions of things went through my mind – the dream Joseph had as a child about stars bowing down before him, the day we beat him up and sold him, the nightmares, the regrets, how deeply sorry I felt for what we, for what I, had done. Joseph looked at me. He said, 'Come closer.' Trembling, I walked closer and felt his powerful arms wrap around my shoulders. I cried.

Joseph was crying too. 'I'm really sorry Joseph,' was all I could say. There was no hint of revenge or bitterness in his eyes, just forgiveness. With a warm smile through the tears, he said, 'What you did was bad, but God has used it for good to save the lives of many people.' We spent the rest of the day with our brother.

I still can't believe that my brother forgave me for all that I had done to him! It was a miracle. Joseph soon sent us home, with a longing in his eyes. He longed to see Dad. I left Egypt that day, determined to bring my father back to the son he thought was lost – the son he loved so much

CONCLUSION
Remind the children of the key word for the day: FORGIVER.

Encourage the children that God is still the Forgiver, and that we can ask God to forgive us the things we do wrong

TESTIMONY
Invite a team member to talk about what they are most impressed by about Joseph as a person. Then let them talk about their own experience of forgiveness, both people they have forgiven or who have forgiven them. Move on to talk about how God can forgive us because of Jesus' death. They need to have thought a lot about how they present that. Look back to the training session on page 29 and on the **PYRAMID ROCK DVD**. Conclude by sharing what it is like to know that we have been forgiven by God. This will be followed up in the Pyramid Groups.

UP THE NILE!
(40 MINUTES)

AT THE OASIS (5 MINUTES)
Serve refreshments in Pyramid Groups.

OPEN THE SCROLLS (10 MINUTES)
For older children
If you are using *Joseph's Jotter*, turn to page 39. Talk about what you might have said to the brothers if you were Joseph and were still really mad with them. To help the children enter into the reality of the situation you could ask them to act out the scene as if they had been angry.

Then unjumble both sets of sentences and check what Joseph actually said by reading Genesis 45:5–8 on page 32. Why do you think Joseph acted like this and not in an angry way? If appropriate, use the prayer on page 41.

If you are not using *Joseph's Jotter*, ask the same questions as above, doing the role play, if appropriate, and then check what Joseph did say in Genesis 45:3–8. On a large sheet of paper, you could write out verse 5 missing out the vowels for the children to complete as a group. Why do you think Joseph acted like this and not in an angry way?

For younger children
On the Pyramid Sheet are written the words Joseph said to his brothers. As you all colour in the picture, talk about how the brothers felt and what Joseph felt. Then talk about how he could forgive them.

For all children
- ▲ When was the last time someone said they forgave you?
- ▲ What sort of things do we find hard to forgive people for?
- ▲ Refer to what was said in the testimony time. You may wish to explain how Jesus forgave the people who had put him to death. In the same way God can forgive us.
- ▲ Share what it means that you know Jesus has forgiven you.

EGYPTIAN GAMES AND CRAFT (25 MINUTES)
Theme-related games and craft (see pages 54–56).

PYRAMID ROCKS!
(35 MINUTES)

MEGA QUESTION
Display today's mega question: 'When was the last time you forgave someone for the wrong things they did to you?' Build on the discussions of the Pyramid Groups.

THE COOL CATS
Either sing the **PYRAMID ROCK** theme song or sing another song with the children.

CAPTAIN KETCHUP'S BIN
Welcome Captain Ketchup back to share some of the contents of his bin! Captain Ketchup should choose a cross section of pictures, jokes and questions. Encourage the children to bring in more for the last day and to make sure they write their name and group on their piece of paper before they pop it in the bin.

MEMORY JOGGER
Ask the children what they can remember of today's programme, including the key word. Sing the memory verse song through a couple of times to help the children remember Stephen's statement. Try to sing it without the words! If you are not using the memory verse song, then see how many children can remember the verse, awarding points, if you are using a points system.

THE ADVENTURES OF DR POTTY:
DR POTTY AND PRINCESS POTTY'S POT PARLOUR
Introduce the continuing adventures of Dr Potty and Denise. Today, Dr Potty and Denise have a mishap with make-up! See today's script on page 43.

CREATIVE PRAYER
Give each child two small pieces of card with the number 4 clearly marked on them, or cut into the shape of a 4. The number 4 signifies 4giveness! Tell the children that you are going to ask God together to forgive you for some of the wrong things you have done. Assure the children that they can ask for forgiveness and that it is an important step in following Jesus.

Suggest that the children think of particular things to say sorry to God for. When prompted they drop first one and then the second of their cards or 4s into the team bucket as a way of showing how God forgives us when we ask him, and takes our guilt away. Then read a prayer similar to the one below, pausing to allow the children to think of things they want to say thank you for.

Some of children may want to pray prayers of commitment and it may be appropriate to encourage them to go to one side with one or two of the leaders to pray with them as outlined in Part 4 (page 26).

Lord, the first thing I want to say sorry for is [pause], so I put this 4 in the bin and I thank you that you forgive me.

Lord, the second thing I want to say sorry for is [pause], so I put this 4 in the bin and I thank you that you forgive me.

THE COOL CATS
Sing the **PYRAMID ROCK** theme song to finish.

PYRAMID GROUPS
(5 MINUTES)

If you are using this, give each child the next Pyramid Piece. Talk about the story so far and what the children think about how Joseph was able to forgive his brothers. Encourage them to keep the Pyramid Pieces safe at home, so they can make up the pyramid at the end of the week. Before they leave, make sure that the children have all their belongings and make sure they are collected by the correct adult.

DAY 4
FORGIVER

Joseph said to his brothers, "Yes, I am your brother, Joseph, the one you sold into Egypt. Don't worry or blame yourselves for what you did. God is the one who sent me ahead of you to save lives." (Genesis 45:4,5)

How many mice can you find in this picture? Colour it in and talk about how Joseph could forgive his brothers.

It is fantastic that God forgives us too. He never stops loving us. Thank God that he does that.

PYRAMID SHEET PHOTOCOPIABLE

DAY 5

KING

AIMS
▲ To show the children that God is the king over all the earth.
▲ To tell the story of how God brought Joseph and his family back together again and how Joseph was sent to Egypt, 'for such a time as this'.

Key story: Joseph and his family are reunited. Joseph looks back on his life and sees God at work. God ultimately brings good from evil.

Key belief: God is the King of all Kings – in control of the nations and the future. He is powerful and good.

Key passage: Genesis 45:25 – 47:12

The world of a child: To understand God's greatness as well as his closeness and friendship is very demanding and may seem strange to some children. It can however be very reassuring to children to realise that God is so big and powerful, in a world that is often very uncertain and frightening.

TEAM PREPARATION
SPIRITUAL PREPARATION
Read together Psalm 105:1,2,12–24.

1 TALK TOGETHER
Briefly discuss these questions:
▲ Write down a list of all the things the psalmist is saying that God did for his people.
▲ Why might the people of Israel call God the Great King?

2 SHARE TOGETHER
God showed in the life of Joseph that he was in ultimate control – the great King. God took Joseph through the difficult times in order to save his people and the lives of many nations.
When Jesus came, he told the people that the kingdom of heaven was near. God was bringing his rule and his reign into people's lives. A Christian is someone who is part of that kingdom – they belong to the King and all they own belongs to the King as well.

Sometimes in life it seems that God is not really in control. Circumstances suggest that God is far away. Heroes of the faith, like Joseph, remind us that God is in ultimate control of the nations. Paul reminds us that one day every knee will bow at the feet of Jesus and worship him (Philippians 2:11).

Be encouraged – the God of Joseph is our God. He rules the nations and he holds the universe in his hands. The world may ignore him, abuse him and walk its own way. The world of education and the media may continue to suggest that there is no God. However, one day we will all bow and acknowledge that God is the great King of the whole world!

3 PRAY TOGETHER
▲ Pray for the day's activities.
▲ Pray for the children in the days and weeks to come and for any follow-up events you have planned.
▲ Pray for the children, that they would really enjoy **PYRAMID ROCK** today.
▲ Pray that the children will get a glimpse of the fact that God is the great King.
▲ Pray for the team, that God will give everyone the strength and stamina to give another 100 per cent today!

PRACTICAL PREPARATIONS
Talk through the morning's programme, and make sure everyone is aware of their responsibilities.

Encourage the team to chat to the children as much as possible. Remind them that Jesus said his kingdom was for children and that he will show his love to them through us! Remind them to talk enthusiastically about any follow-up events.

Ensure that all the resources are ready for the various activities.

EQUIPMENT CHECKLIST – DAY 5
SECURITY registration forms, badges, pens, team lists
PYRAMID GROUPS badges, pens, Bibles, Joseph's Jotters, Pyramid Sheets, Open the scroll resources, flip-chart paper, Pyramid Pieces, spare paper
MUSIC music for your chosen songs, including the **PYRAMID ROCK** theme song, and other background music
DRAMA costumes and props
TECHNOLOGY check PA, OHP/data projector and DVD player are working and in focus, check you have all visuals needed on acetate or PowerPoint
ACTIVITIES all equipment needed for games and craft
HOLIDAY CLUB LEADER running order, notes and key word flashcard
CREATIVE PRAYER prayer on PowerPoint or acetate
REFRESHMENTS drinks and biscuits, or other snacks
TEACHING PYRAMID ROCK DVD and/or Joseph costume

PROGRAMME

PYRAMID GROUP WELCOME
(10 MINUTES)

Play some lively music and display the **PYRAMID ROCK** logo to welcome the children as they arrive and are registered. Each child should be given their badge for the day. Ask the children what they have enjoyed this week and what they have learnt about God. Pyramid Leaders should encourage the children to complete their pyramids when they get home and to bring them back to the family service/party at the end of the week.

RED HOT!
(45 MINUTES)

HOLIDAY CLUB LEADER WELCOME
Ask the children if they can remember all four key words and what the order was. State that, through the story of Joseph, we have been building up a picture of how wonderful the God of Joseph is!

KEY WORD
Display the key word, and at the same time display a small flashcard with the key word on it at the front of the room.

Day 5: KING
Ask the children what the word means. (*Ruler of a kingdom. The land, the people and the power belong to him.*)

Reveal, or write up, the meaning of the key word. State that this is the key word for today and encourage the children to see how it fits into our programme!

BOUNCING BENJAMIN
Introduce Benjamin and the day's aerobic work-out. Try to run a royal theme through the work-out!

JOSEPH MEGA-GAME – TRAVEL KIT!
The Holiday Club Leader introduces the rules of today's game, entitled *Travel Kit!*

Today's picture is a set of 14 pictures, showing some of the items you will need to take with you if you are going on a long trip, much like Joseph's family had to do to get from Canaan to Egypt (see page 53 or the **PYRAMID ROCK** website). The Holiday Club Leader shows the picture for 60 seconds to show the pictures. The children write down in their Pyramid Groups all the items they can remember. The Holiday Club Leader reveals the pictures again, with the Pyramid Leaders marking their team's sheets. Award points for correct answers, if you are using a points system.

THE COOL CATS
Sing the **PYRAMID ROCK** theme song.

RED HOT NEWS – WITH CAPTAIN KETCHUP

The Holiday Club Leader welcomes the children to the Red Hot Newsroom, and asks them to welcome Captain Ketchup, who is going to read today's news. Everyone should jump up to do the Captain Ketchup dance at the appropriate moment. You may want to add artefacts such as a cup and a sack. You will need additional pictures.

Captain Ketchup Good morning, everyone, and welcome to the Red Hot NewsDesk – let's do the Ketchup dance! (Do the Ketchup dance with CK joining in! Then all sit down and focus on CK. The news today should be read at super-speed!) Here is the very latest on the dramatic story of Joseph.

Joseph was sold as a slave by his brothers and taken to Egypt. They were fed up with him and his crazy dreams!

Joseph was sold to Potiphar, the Captain of the Guard.

Joseph then ended up in prison for a few years, until..

Pharaoh had a dream about the famine!

Joseph was promoted to the position of Prime Minister and he ruled the land.

Amazingly Joseph's brothers turned up in Egypt desperate for food.

Joseph tested them by planting his golden cup in Benjamin's bag.

When Joseph saw that they had changed, and how upset they were that they had got rid of him, Joseph told them who he was. Everyone who saw it was amazed by Joseph because he forgave his brothers for everything they had done. Joseph sent his brothers home to get his really, really, really old dad to come down to Egypt.

But, will Jacob make it? Will Joseph be reunited with his long lost dad? What was Joseph thinking as he waited for his family to come to Egypt?

At this point, either show Episode Five of the **PYRAMID ROCK DVD** and/or continue with Captain Ketchup and the key witness (Joseph) monologue:

KEY WITNESS: JOSEPH

Holiday Club Leader Great questions. Hello, Captain Ketchup. I wonder what Joseph was really thinking!?

Captain Ketchup I reckon he was thinking, 'I wanna see my dad!'

Holiday Club Leader I think there were probably lots of thoughts going around his brain! I don't suppose you've got another one of your expert witnesses in the studio have you?!

Captain Ketchup Funny you should ask, cos here comes Joseph himself!

Joseph stumbles in, as though thrown in through a time machine.

Joseph One day, I found myself sitting on the wall near my office in Egypt lost in my thoughts. I remembered sitting on my dad's knee, a small, happy boy. He would tell me of how God had promised to him, to my grandad, and to my great-grandad, that our family would grow to be a mighty nation.

Then I thought about how God had used me to save the lives of the nation of Egypt, and now my own family.

I began to picture the face of my father. I had thought about my father so many times during the previous 22 years.

It was 22 long years. I had worked in the house of Potiphar, spent cold, long nights in that lonely prison, and now I ruled Egypt as Prime Minister. It was 22 years without my father, but it was 22 years with a loving God. I knew God had created me and made me for a reason – that was now very clear to me. I knew that he was with me and that he was my helper – I learned that as a slave. God had provided me with so much – and now, through me, provided everyone in the countries around us with food to eat. I knew his forgiveness as I battled with my feelings. I had forgiven my brothers and asked God to take away the resentment and pain I felt.

Then, as I looked back on my life, I prayed.

I thanked God for my family. I thanked him that even though my brothers had been so cruel, that God had used my life for good. I thanked him that Pharaoh was in control of Egypt and that God was in control of the whole world! I thanked him that I belonged to him and that he was my King. Lastly, I thanked him that I was going to see my dad again.

After Judah had left, I prayed every day that God would help my father, who was so old, to make the journey from Canaan. I'd arranged with Pharaoh that my family could stay in Goshen, a really nice part of Egypt, where I would be able to care for them and provide them with the food they needed to survive.

Then came the most fantastic day, the day I saw and hugged my father again. One of my soldiers told me that my family was near. I got into my special chariot and rode like the wind to meet them. Then, a few kilometres outside Egypt, I saw my father. It really was him. Happiness bubbled up inside. It's hard to describe.

We had some good times after that. I really got to know and love my brothers again. We had some great feasts and we had some wacky fun! My two sons, Manasseh and Ephraim, got to know all the children of my brothers. We were now a very big family – 70 in all. Not quite a nation yet, but we are on our way!

I'm still the Prime Minister in Egypt but I really serve the King of the whole earth.

It's been great to meet you all.

CONCLUSION
Remind the children about the key word for the day: KING

Look back over the key words because they will help us understand what sort of King God is.

PLANNER He made you and has a plan for you.
HELPER He promises to be with you and to help you.
PROVIDER He promises to provide for all your needs because he cares for you.
FORGIVER He promises to forgive you through the death of his son, Jesus.
KING He is in overall control and he wants you to belong to him.

Encourage the children that God is the King of all. A Christian is someone who has decided to belong to the King. God wants everyone to be part of his special, wonderful kingdom.

UP THE NILE!
(40 MINUTES)

AT THE OASIS (5 MINUTES)
You could provide something extra special as Jacob and his father were reunited!

OPEN THE SCROLL (10 MINUTES)
For older children
If you are using *Joseph's Jotter*, turn to page 43 and write or draw the imaginary postcard Joseph wrote to his dad, Jacob. Then read Genesis 46:1–4 on page 35. Read it out loud with one child as narrator, one child as God and one child as Jacob. On page 44, write down all the things God says he will do for Jacob.

If you are not using *Joseph's Jotter*, read Genesis 46:1–4 as above and give the children a card to use as an imaginary postcard, to write as if they are Joseph inviting Jacob to come to Egypt. Then write down on a piece of flip-chart paper all that God said he would do for Jacob.

For younger children
There is a similar postcard on the Pyramid Sheet which explores Genesis 46:3.

For all children
Make a list of all the things God has done for us.

▲ Talk about how some of these things have affected other people. For example, a baby brother or sister affects our life in lots of ways; or being ill then getting better. Relate it to Joseph's attitude to his life's troubles.
▲ Share examples from your own life.

You may want to thank God for all he has done for us. If any child wants to know how they can personally know God's care and forgiveness, find time to pray and talk with them too.

EGYPTIAN GAMES AND CRAFTS (25 MINUTES)
Theme-related games and craft (see pages 54–56).

PYRAMID ROCKS!
(40 MINUTES)

MEGA QUESTION
Ask today's mega question: 'Make a list of things that belong to a king!'

TESTIMONY
Ask a team member to talk briefly about how God has been in control of their lives. They should be encouraged to talk about some recent experiences that have shown God at work. Talk about Jesus being there with them.

Ask the children if they can think of times when they think God was in control of their lives. Joseph was able to look back and see that God had been with him every step of the way, bringing good from a very bad situation. Pyramid Leaders could share from their group discussions.

THE COOL CATS
Either sing the **PYRAMID ROCK** theme song or sing another song with the children.

CAPTAIN KETCHUP'S BIN
Welcome Captain Ketchup back to share some of the contents of his bin! Captain Ketchup should choose a selection of pictures, jokes and questions. Thank the children for all their contributions to the Captain Ketchup bin this week!

MEMORY JOGGER
Ask the children what they can remember of today's programme, particularly the key word for each day. Who can remember the memory verse? Sing the song together, if you have used it, or ask for a volunteer from each Pyramid Group to come up to the front and say the verse.

THE ADVENTURES OF DR POTTY:
DR POTTY AND THE TOMB OF FACIAL RESTORATION

Introduce the continuing adventures of Dr Potty and Denise. Today they finally make an important discovery! See today's script on page 45.

CREATIVE PRAYER

Encourage the children that knowing, following and learning about Jesus doesn't end here! The best way to follow Jesus is with other people's help, and as part of a group. Invite the children to come to your children's group/church/family service. Make sure they know about follow-up events and clubs.

To finish **PYRAMID ROCK** today, tell the children that you are going to pray together. Show this simple prayer. In the Bible, it encourages us to shout to God! So encourage the children that, sensibly, but with enjoyment, they can shout this prayer to God.

> Thank you great big loving God,
> That you're alive today,
> We have learnt how great you are,
> Like Joseph used to say!
>
> Thank you great big loving God,
> For everything we've done,
> For all the team and all who've helped,
> To make this week such fun!
>
> Thank you Lord for **PYRAMID ROCK!**
> Amen.

THE COOL CATS

Sing the **PYRAMID ROCK** theme song to finish.

PYRAMID GROUPS
(5 MINUTES)

If you are using them, give the children the final Pyramid Piece and then encourage them to construct the pyramid by following the instructions given on the sheets, using the other pieces at home. If any child has brought all the Pyramid Pieces to the club, find time to help them construct it. Remind the children that they could bring their completed pyramids to the family service/party for judging in a special 'Joseph Pyramid Competition'. Thank the children for coming to **PYRAMID ROCK** and for making it such an exciting time. Children should collect their belongings ready for going home. Make sure they are collected by the correct adult.

DAY 5
KING

God said to Jacob, "I am God, the same God your father worshipped. Don't be afraid to go to Egypt ... I will go with you to Egypt and later I will bring your descendants back here." (Genesis 46:3,4)

Draw a wavy line under what God said he would do for Jacob.

Write down what Joseph would write to his dad, inviting him to come to Egypt. Or you could draw a picture Joseph might send to his dad.

Dear Dad,

Joseph

PHARAOH'S FINEST POSTCARDS
Egypt's favourite funny cards brought to you by Egypt's favourite Pharaoh

My dad, Jacob
Canaan
A long way from Egypt

Joseph and his dad, Jacob, both knew that God was with them. God is the King of the whole world. He has done so much for us!

What is the best thing about Pyramid Rock? Thank God for that.

PYRAMID SHEET
PHOTOCOPIABLE

SUNDAY 2

FAMILY SERVICE OUTLINE

FORGIVENESS IS FOREVER

AIM

▲ To review all the teaching and fun of the club for everyone's benefit, children, families and the rest of the church.

Key story: After Jacob's death, Joseph reassures his brothers that they are forgiven.

Key link to the holiday club: During the holiday club we have looked closely at the amazing story of Joseph. We have seen God bring good from evil and we have seen Joseph's commitment to being faithful to God.

Key passage: Genesis 50:15–26

SERVICE OUTLINE

FEEDBACK
The Holiday Club Leader should report back to the congregation on how the holiday club has gone. Relate how God has answered your prayers. Share the highs and the lows, and the challenges that you now face as a church. Particularly welcome the children and their families who have come to church for the first time today.

SONGS
Ask the band, The Cool Cats, to lead the congregation in the **PYRAMID ROCK** theme song. (Alternatively, use the song from the DVD.)

THE ADVENTURES OF DR POTTY: DR POTTY AND THE ANCIENT RELIC
Dr Potty and Denise, with the help of the church leader, relive the action from this week's dramas! (See page 46 for the script.)

JOSEPH MEGA-GAME
Choose one of the Joseph mega-games that were played this week, and challenge the church to do as well as the children.

RED HOT NEWS – WITH CAPTAIN KETCHUP
Introduce everyone to Captain Ketchup, who has been reading the Red Hot News this week! (Don't forget the Ketchup dance!) You might want to add a large postcard like the one children made on Day 5.

Captain Ketchup Good morning everyone and welcome to the Red Hot News Desk – let's do the Ketchup dance! (Do the Ketchup dance!) Here is the very latest on the dramatic story of Joseph.
   Joseph was sold as a slave by his brothers and taken to Egypt. They were fed up with him and his crazy dreams!

Joseph was sold to Potiphar, Captain of the Guard.

Joseph then ended up in prison for a few years, until…

Pharaoh had a dream about the famine!

Joseph was promoted to the position of Prime Minister and he ruled the land.

Amazingly Joseph's brothers turned up in Egypt desperate for food.

Joseph tested them by planting his golden cup in Benjamin's bag.

When Joseph saw that they had changed, and how upset they were that they had got rid of him, Joseph told them who he was. Everyone who saw it was amazed by Joseph because he forgave his brothers for everything they had done.

Joseph sent his brothers home to get all the family and bring them down to Egypt, so that (with God's help) Joseph could look after them.

There were emotional scenes when Joseph spotted his dad, and went to meet him in his posh chariot. For the first time in over twenty years they hugged each other and cried!

And so this story has a happy ending. There have been reports, however, that 17 years later Jacob is going to die!

Holiday Club Leader Really? Hello Captain Ketchup. Is it really true that Jacob is dying?

Captain Ketchup He is a very old man – about 147!

Holiday Club Leader I wonder what will happen when he does die?!

Captain Ketchup Tell you what, why don't you read what happens in Genesis chapter 50! I've got to go… I'm getting too hot in the Red Hot News Desk today! Bye!

BIBLE READING

Some good readers read Genesis 50:15–21 as a narrative with appropriate miming. Then read Genesis 22:17.

TEACHING

Briefly go over the events of the story you have just read. Jacob died, after blessing his sons and adopting the two sons of Joseph. Jacob also made Joseph promise to bury him with his father Isaac and his grandfather Abraham. Then Jacob died and everyone was really sad. After burying Jacob in Canaan, with the help of all his brothers and a lot of Egyptians, everyone returned to Egypt. The brothers though, still felt guilty for what they did to Joseph and worried that, now Jacob was dead, Joseph might punish them.

Joseph, once again, acted in a way that pleased God. He wept at the request for forgiveness and he watched his brothers throw themselves at his feet, an act foretold in the dream of his youth. Then Joseph 'reassured them and spoke kindly to them' (verse 21, NIV). He reminded his brothers that God had brought good from all the sin. Joseph had saved many lives through coming to Egypt.

Show the congregation the acorn and the small oak tree used in Family Service A. See if they can remember why these were used in the last service. State that God took Abraham (acorn or seed), and by the time it got to the beginning of the story of Joseph there were 17 people in the family. By the time Jacob came to Egypt there were at least 70 in the family (Genesis 46:27). Ask the congregation how long the people of Israel stayed in Egypt. The answer is 400 years, and when they came out there were between two and three million of them! It was as if Egypt was the best place to plant his small oak tree to see it grow into a massive, strong tree. Moses led the people back to the land of Canaan, to form the nation of Israel. (You might find it helpful to put a map on the screen as you talk about these things.)

So the story today reminds us of two things that were true for Joseph and are true today.
Firstly – Joseph knew God's care which helped him forgive his brothers. Even more so, God has forgiven us because of what Jesus has done. That means he can also help us to forgive others (Peter states in 1 Peter 3:18 that Christ died for sin, once and for all in order to lead us to God).
Secondly – God has a plan for the whole world, which included Joseph 4,000 years ago and includes us today!

PRAYER

Spend some time thanking God for **PYRAMID ROCK**. Encourage some of the children who have taken part during the week to come to the front and pray. This may need to be prepared before the service. Include thanking God for everyone who took part in **PYRAMID ROCK** and helped to make it a success.

CONCLUDE

Choose some songs which visitors may be familiar with.

PART 8
OTHER WAYS TO USE PYRAMID ROCK?

FOLLOW-UP IDEAS

PYRAMID ROCK doesn't have to finish at the end of the week! Here are a few suggestions for follow-up ideas:

ROCKY ROAD

Rocky Road is material written for midweek and weekend children's clubs specifically to follow on from Joseph, although it can be used by churches or groups who have not done this holiday club. The programme explores the story of Moses, when Joseph and his family were a distant memory, and the Israelites were enslaved by the Egyptians. It contains ten sessions which give you everything you need to run such a club with non-churched children in mind.

OTHER EYE LEVEL CLUBS

Rocky Road is just one of Scripture Union's midweek *eye level* club programmes, designed to help you work with non-churched children.

Streetwise follows Jesus as he visits different people's houses, as told by Luke. The *Streetwise* DVD accompanies the programme (the *Luke Street* video can be used). The DVD also contains resource material and the *Streetwise* song.

Awesome! looks at signs of Jesus as described by John. The *Awesome!* DVD links in with this programme (the *Signposts* video can be used). The DVD also contains resource material and the *Awesome!* song.

Clues2Use is a follow-up club to *Landlubbers*, but can also be used on its own. It is accompanied by *The Jesus Quest* DVD.

ADAPTING PYRAMID ROCK FOR A WEEKLY CLUB

A weekly club usually has the following limitations:
▲ Less time together.
▲ A smaller team.
▲ Less time to prepare.
▲ Less flexibility in preparing the venue.

A weekly club has the following benefits:
▲ Ongoing relationship building with both children and families.
▲ Less time required in one particular week.
▲ Children who could not make a holiday club will be able to come.
▲ Leaders who are only available in the evenings/on Saturdays can help.

ADAPTING THE MATERIAL

Here are a few guidelines on how to adapt one of the **PYRAMID ROCK** daily outlines:
▲ Work out how much you can realistically fit into the time available.
▲ Make sure you tell the story clearly, either using the DVD or with the characters from the story appearing live.
▲ Allow time for children to unpack the story's meaning in smaller groups.
▲ The story of Joseph covers about 14 chapters in Genesis. It would easily be split into enough stories to cover a term's worth of meetings.

ADAPTING PYRAMID ROCK FOR USE WITH OTHER AGE-RANGES

PYRAMID ROCK has been specifically written for use with children between the ages of 5 and 11. However, you could adapt it for different age groups.

PART 8 · OTHER WAYS TO USE PYRAMID ROCK?

Adults

In preparation for the holiday club, why not run an adult teaching programme on Joseph's life. SU publish a Lifebuilder small-group resource based on the story of Joseph.

A whole series of adult talks can be put together following the amazing story of Joseph and the people of Israel.

Youth

The story of Joseph is packed with issues relevant to young people. Joseph starts the story with a high level of arrogance, when he tells his brothers his dreams. He then has to deal with betrayal, hope, love, sexual temptation, leadership issues, living for God when no one else believes in the same God. You may wish to even take the five-day story structure of **PYRAMID ROCK**, and adapt the discussion to the level of the young people. Young people sometimes relate to puppets too, so you may find Captain Ketchup is a big hit! It would be great to have as many young people as possible involved as young leaders in **PYRAMID ROCK**!

Pre-school

You could make some provision for pre-school children in your **PYRAMID ROCK** week. Providing a room for parents with toddlers, with tea and coffee available, can make your club more inviting, and can give you the opportunity to develop relationships with the parents of the children who come. The **PYRAMID ROCK** programme is not geared to children of this age. Although with some creativity anything is possible, bringing them into the main programme will change the nature of the programme, make things more difficult to run and may discourage some of the older children from coming.

The *Tiddlywinks* series, published by Scripture Union, provides a wide range of material to use with under-5s. The eight *Big Books* provide material for use in groups – parent and toddler groups, Sunday groups or other situations – providing stories, games, rhymes and more to help children explore a Bible passage in an age-appropriate way. The eight accompanying *Little Books* provide a way to think about the Bible at home, with parents or carers looking at a story and Bible passage with their child.

OTHER IDEAS

▲ A **PYRAMID ROCK** Egypt party – an early evening event for all the family to enjoy. This could fit nicely on to the end of the **PYRAMID ROCK** week.

▲ A series of church meetings exploring the history of the people of Israel.

▲ A small **PYRAMID ROCK** cell group for those children who have shown particular interest and want to discover more. Visit the Scripture Union website for details of materials to use for this.

▲ Stay in touch with the children by personally delivering Christmas and Easter cards.

▲ Plan a carol service with **PYRAMID ROCK** children in mind. For ideas of other Christmas events for children outside the church, get hold of *Christmas Wrapped Up!* – visit the Scripture Union website to find out more details.

▲ Plan Easter events for **PYRAMID ROCK** children and their families. *Easter Cracked* is full of great ideas.

▲ Plan an event as an alternative to Halloween.

CONSIDER WORKING WITH YOUR LOCAL PRIMARY SCHOOL

▲ You could provide *It's Your Move!*, the book for children moving on to secondary school, or *Get Ready Go!*, for children starting school.

▲ You could offer to take an assembly or RE lesson, or help out in any other way. Primary schools usually welcome suitable adult help.

£5 OFF!

BUY £60 WORTH OF EXTRA PYRAMID ROCK RESOURCES AND GET £5 OFF!

Redeem your voucher as follows:

1 Take to your local Christian Bookshop

2 Send to Scripture Union Mail Order, PO Box 5148, Milton Keynes MLO, MK2 2YX with your order and payment

3 Visit our online shop at www.scriptureunion.org.uk and place your order online where the £5 discount will be applied

WORKING WITH FAMILIES

Children, of course, are part of a much wider family network. If we want to see children grow in their faith in Jesus, we need to recognise that family members may not always understand, or sympathise with, the teaching and purpose of any outreach to children. However, they themselves need to talk about a need to know Christ too!

- Make sure that family members are well informed about what has happened during the club and also that they know what is planned in the weeks to come.
- Explore ways of building good relationships with the family – such as a treasure hunt, football training, a Christmas party for the whole family.
- Parenting courses, a men's and women's breakfast or holiday clubs for the elderly are just some examples of meeting genuine adult needs and building relationships.
- Some family members may be ready for a more specifically Christian exploration or discipleship event/course.
- Older siblings who have attended a holiday club in the past often feel nostalgic when a local holiday club is running. Is this a short-lived opportunity to build bridges?

AND FINALLY…

How has your team of leaders developed over the period of the holiday club? Did obvious training needs become apparent?

- Consider setting up a training session (or more than one) to develop the abilities of the team. You could open this out to other churches in your area. There may already be training events in your area – contact SU for further details.
- Encourage your holiday club prayer group to keep praying, updating them regularly.
- Identify any gaps in the leadership of your regular children's programme and invite **PYRAMID ROCK** team members to get involved.

Many holiday clubs are the key time in the year when children's workers are at their most creative and most daring! It would be impossible to sustain that level of activity for the rest of the year but the same spirit of risk and innovation could be sustained! Dream dreams and see what God makes happen!

This voucher cannot be exchanged for cash or any other merchandise and cannot be used with any other offer. This offer includes the **PYRAMID ROCK** resource book, DVD and *Joseph's Jotter* (singles and packs). It does not include CPO publicity merchandise. Only single orders of £60 and above qualify for this offer.

TO THE RETAILER: Please accept this voucher as a discount payment.
CREDIT DUE: £5.00 less normal trade discount.
This voucher must be returned to:
STL Customer Services, PO Box 300,
Carlisle, Cumbria, CA3 0QS by 1st September 2006.

NAME OF SHOP: _____

STL ACCOUNT NUMBER: _____

VOPRHC

PART 8 · OTHER WAYS TO USE PYRAMID ROCK?

JOIN US ON OUR JOURNEY!

Many people tells us at Scripture Union about how they have used our holiday club material, what worked or what didn't, and how God blessed them in their club. We really welcome any feedback we receive and it excites us as we go on this journey together of sharing the good news of Jesus with children. If you could, we would love you to complete this form and send it to us. Alternatively, you could email us your responses to holidayclub@scriptureunion.org.uk

PYRAMID ROCK FEEDBACK FORM

Name

Address

Church name

Church address

Numbers of children at **PYRAMID ROCK**

5 to 7s

8 to 11s

Other age groups (please specify)

In your opinion, what was the ratio of churched/non-churched children?

What comments do you have about how your club went?

What comments do you have about the **PYRAMID ROCK** material?

What plans for following up **PYRAMID ROCK** do you have? How will you keep in contact with the children and their families?

What two training needs do you think you have in your team

Is there any way Scripture Union could help you in your children's work?

☐ We would like to keep in touch with you by placing your name on our mailing list. If you would prefer not to be added, please tick the box. SU does not sell or lease its mailing list.